FIRST SATURDAY DEVOTIONS TO MARY:
A HANDBOOK

Visit our web site at
www.albahouse.org
(for orders www.stpauls.us)
or call 1-800-343-2522 (ALBA)
and request current catalog

FIRST SATURDAY DEVOTIONS TO MARY: A HANDBOOK

Deacon Roy Barkley

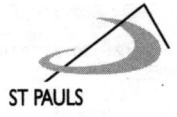

Library of Congress Cataloging-in-Publication Data

Barkley, Roy.
  First Saturday devotions to Mary: a handbook / by Roy Barkley.
     p. cm.
  ISBN 0-8189-1243-X
  1. Mary, Blessed Virgin, Saint—Devotion to—Portugal—Fatima. 2. Fatima, Our Lady of. I. Title.

BT660.F3B235   2007
232.91—dc22

2006031645

Produced and designed in the United States of America by the
Fathers and Brothers of the Society of St. Paul,
2187 Victory Boulevard, Staten Island, New York 10314-6603,
as part of their communications apostolate. Printed in Canada.

ISBN 0-8189-1243-X
ISBN 978-0-8189-1243-6

© Copyright 2007 by the Society of St. Paul / Alba House

Printing Information:

Current Printing - first digit	1	2	3	4	5	6	7	8	9	10
Year of Current Printing - first year shown										
2007	2008	2009	2010	2011	2012	2013	2014	2015	2016	

Contents

Preface vii

The First Saturday Devotion: What It Includes and
    What It Promises 1
    The Parts 3
    The Promises 8

Reflections on the Twenty Mysteries of the Rosary 9
    Introduction to the Rosary 11
    How to Use this Book in Saying the Rosary 16
    The Joyful Mysteries 19
    The Luminous Mysteries 41
    The Sorrowful Mysteries 65
    The Glorious Mysteries 87

Reflections Before the Blessed Sacrament 107

Confession 141
    Why Do Penance? 143
    On Conscience and the Commandments 147
    How to Confess 150
    Examination of Conscience in Light of the
    Ten Commandments 155
    Commandment 1 156
    Commandment 2 159
    Commandment 3 162
    Commandment 4 165
    Commandment 5 169
    Commandment 6 175
    Commandment 7 183
    Commandment 8 189
    Commandment 9 193
    Commandment 10 196

A Blessing 200

Preface

My purposes in this book are
- to add depth to Marian devotions, specifically the First Saturday Devotion;
- and in so doing, to aid the reader in making reparations to her Immaculate Heart.

To achieve these goals, I offer reflections on the elements of the First Saturday Devotion — the mysteries of the Rosary, the sacrament of Penance, and the Eucharist — and practical suggestions about them. The reflections on Penance principally comprise an examination of conscience based on the Ten Commandments. The eucharistic meditations focus on various aspects of the Eucharist, especially as these relate to Mary and the Rosary.

I am well aware that a book like this is too much to use very thoroughly on a given Saturday morning. But such use is not my intent. When we take part in any kind of regular devotion, we are participating in the holiness of God and His saints. We are not as interested then in explanations and definitions as we are in silent awareness of God's presence and His gifts. The explanations come mainly at other times. When I am at Mass or kneeling before the Blessed Sacrament, I want a little theology but a lot of worship. Theological reflection is related to devotion somewhat as practice is to performance. When we are not actually worshiping, we can reflect at length on the meaning of a given mystery or aspect of God's grace, and this reflection adds depth to our devotional time and thoughts. When we're worshiping, we're not studying.

So my hope is that this book will enrich the reader's understanding, but not at the expense of worship. Toward that end, I recommend reading the reflections on only one mystery during a particular Rosary; on only one of the Ten Commandments before a given confession. Afterwards, and before the next First Saturday, you can read and reflect on the book at length.

The reflections offered here are based on documents of central importance in the Church — the *Catechism of the Catholic Church*, with occasional reference to its forbear, the *Catechism of the Council of Trent*, and to other magisterial writings; and the Scriptures — as well as on my own contemplation of God's words and works. The scriptural passages come from the Revised Standard Version unless otherwise noted.

The First Saturday Devotion:
What It Includes and What It Promises

Look, my daughter, at my heart encircled with thorns, with which ungrateful men wound it every moment by their blasphemies and ingratitude. Give me consolation, you, at least; and announce for me that I promise to assist at the hour of death, with the graces necessary for salvation, all who on the first Saturday of five consecutive months confess, receive Holy Communion, recite five decades of the Rosary, and keep me company for fifteen minutes meditating on the mysteries of the Rosary, with the purpose of making reparation to me.

The Blessed Virgin speaks to Sister Lucia of Fatima,
December 10, 1925

THUS DOES OUR LADY SUMMARIZE THE PARTS
AND THE PROMISES OF THE FIRST SATURDAY DEVOTION.

The Parts

At Fatima Mary asked the blessed children to announce a special devotion to be carried out on five consecutive First Saturdays. This spiritual exercise is to include Confession, the Rosary with meditation on the mysteries, and Mass and Holy Communion. The specific purpose is to make reparation to the Immaculate Heart of Mary. From carrying out the devotion, we can receive all the blessings that come to us through the Woman who brought the Incarnate God into the world. These blessings include wonderful promises of spiritual help.

Five consecutive First Saturdays. The Church makes clear enough that most open Saturdays — Saturdays that are not feast days — are to be devoted to the Blessed Virgin, just as Sundays are devoted to the memory of her Son's Resurrection from the dead and to all that goes into the offering of Holy Mass. The Mass has readings, and the *Divine Office* has special parts, designated "Blessed Virgin Mary on Saturday." Though Fatima gave impetus to this celebration, honoring Mary on Saturday was already a part of the Church's practice. What Mary asked the blessed children of Fatima was that the First Saturday be set aside with more deliberation and attention than formerly — especially as an act of reparation to her Immaculate Heart. You can be devoted to Mary without observing the First Saturdays, but you can't be devoted to her without *some* effort. Surely the attentive offering of five consecutive First Saturdays to Our Lady is the sign of such an effort. It bespeaks devotion to her. And devotion to Mary is required of Catholics. The Blessed Mother's prayer, and the Church's, and mine, is that our devotion to her will be daily and permanent. Toward a life in the constant company of the Blessed Virgin and her Firstborn Son — that is where the five First Saturdays point.

Confession. The Sacrament of Penance has fallen into pitiful disuse. Catholics have followed the lead of the modern West. They have listened to the gospel of self-esteem so well that they no longer think they are in need of contrition before God. "I'm okay, you're okay" is the new creed. And, we might add, God is okay too as long as He stays in His place and approves what we do. Young people living in blatant disobedience to the Ten Commandments — perhaps particularly the Sixth and the Ninth — confidently assert that they have done nothing wrong. Older people have settled into the deceptive comfort of doing as they wish and simply not sweating what God thinks. Many can no longer conceive that He might disapprove of their actions. They are far from understanding that they construct themselves morally and spiritually by their thoughts, words, and deeds; and that they may be building a self that won't fit in heaven. "I'm okay." Against this very unrealistic spiritual self-concept the Blessed Virgin insists upon confession, contrition, and penance for our sins. The biblical teaching on this matter is very clear, as is the teaching of the Church: "All have sinned and fallen short of the glory of God" (Romans 3:23). Without sorrow for sins there is no forgiveness. And so Our Lady asks us to go to Confession once a month, on the First Saturday or within eight days before or after the First Saturday. In doing so, we receive the cleansing from spiritual dirt that will make us fit to receive her Son in Holy Communion and to be in her presence.

Holy Communion. The Blessed Virgin is Mother of the Eucharist, as the Church teaches. Jesus Christ, her Firstborn, Son of Mary and Son of God, instituted the Holy Sacrifice of the Mass as the sign and means of His perpetual presence in His Church.

The First Saturday Devotion

On the altars of the Catholic Church, Jesus keeps His promise to transform bread and wine into His Body and Blood. Those holy elements found their first earthly reality in the womb of the Blessed Virgin. Transformed by His Resurrection, Jesus abides — body, blood, soul, spirit, humanity, divinity — in the sacred species nurtured by the Virgin's blood. Though she remained the humble handmaid of the Lord, even after His glorious victory over death, she must have felt the magnitude of her role in salvation as she saw the very Body and Blood of her Son confected on the altars of the Church, and herself received that divine Food from those altars. She is Mother of the Eucharist indeed, and our Mother in faith. We commune with Jesus Christ in receiving Holy Communion, but we also commune with her who formed Him in her womb. Because of her special relation to the Eucharist, this book includes a handful of eucharistic reflections in addition to the reflections on the mysteries of the Rosary. I hope that readers will use these reflections to enter into a special communion with Our Lady, with Christ's Body the Church, and with the divinizing power of our Creator Himself.

Recitation of the Rosary with reflection on the mysteries. Those who say the Rosary daily and reflect on the mysteries have in their consciousness a steady reminder of the main events of salvation history. For the mysteries are nothing but episodes from the life of Jesus, our Savior, as refracted mostly through the eyes of Mary, who brought Him to us. Whence the Rosary? There was a time — a very long time — during which most members of the Church could not read. That was well enough, for books weren't available anyway. In such a situation, a memorized list of biblical events was a wonderful way for the laity to learn and review the deeds of Christ and the Virgin. The Rosary was both catechism and devotion. In our time most of the laity know how to read, and books are so commonplace that they are often worth little. But our need for daily reflection on the life of Christ

— how God became man, proclaimed the Kingdom, suffered a cruel death, conquered sin and hell, and returned to His Father — is just as pressing as it ever was. How many people actually read the Scriptures daily? How many practice *lectio divina*, the Scripture reading that is also prayer and reflection? How much contemplation of God's word are we able to fit into the demands of modern living? One of the great things about the Rosary is that using it — praying it — can be fitted into daily time that would otherwise be empty. The reflections on the Rosary in this book offer content for this great prayer. I claim no originality for them, but merely that they have come from a lifetime in the presence of Jesus and Mary (a presence of which I have always been clearly unworthy). When the Blessed Virgin asks us to stop for a while in church and reflect on the Jesus that she knew on earth and still knows in heaven, let us respond with joy and faith. These First Saturday reflections, though formally like those of the Rosary we say while driving to work or waiting somewhere for something, are set aside especially for our Mother in faith. Let us be with her in the presence of the Lord.

Amends to the Immaculate Heart. One of our purposes in keeping the First Saturdays is to make reparation to the Immaculate Heart of Mary for sins against her Son and hence against her. Strictly speaking, of course, all sin is an offense against God. If I hurt my friend, the injury is not a sin against him but a painful affront for which I must ask forgiveness. The sin as such is against God. Furthermore, if I witness an injurious act between two other people, forgiveness is out of my power. They must forgive each other, and only God can forgive the sin involved. Sin is by definition a thought, word, or deed that makes one unfit for God's presence. Mary is our friend and Mother, and we have often hurt her. She wants us to be in perfect reconciliation with the Father through her divine Son. When we commit any kind of sin, we violate her loving, maternal will for us. What an honor that she still loves us and prays for us. And what a duty we have to make amends to her who, next to Jesus, is our best friend and most constant helper. In the First Saturday Devotion, we make amends to her especially for five insults: denial of her Immaculate Conception; denial of her perpetual virginity; denial of her divine maternity or her motherhood of the human race; teaching children indifference, contempt, or hatred for the Blessed Virgin; or insulting her in her sacred images. (In recent years, who has not seen or heard of blasphemously disfigured, mocking images of Mary? We should tremble.) So we offer our devotion to her whom we have hurt.

The Promises

Those who keep five consecutive First Saturdays have these promises from Our Lady:

> **That** she will be present at the hour of their death, and assist them with saving graces.
> We should always pray for the dying — that Mary will meet them, and that she will show them, as the *Salve Regina* requests, the "blessed fruit" of her womb, Jesus. Even if my journey from earth to heaven involves a long sojourn in purgatory, it is wonderful to know that Mary will be helping me — leading me toward the Beatific Vision and an eternity of perfect happiness.
> What could be more important?
> **That** souls will be saved and peace will grow when we promote, by word and deed, devotion to the Immaculate Heart.

Let us return the love of the Blessed Virgin because she is worthy of our affection, devotion, and service, and not in order to receive a reward. But let us also rest in the knowledge that devotion to Our Lady brings the assurance of joy beyond our imagination.

Reflections on the Twenty Mysteries of the Rosary

Our Lady asks us to say the Rosary publicly
and, as an adjunct, to reflect on a set
of five mysteries —
Joyful,
Luminous,
Sorrowful,
or Glorious.

Introduction to the Rosary

Mary asked at Fatima that we pray the Rosary and reflect on its mysteries. This is one of the major components of the First Saturday Devotion. But there is more to this great prayer than merely saying so many *Our Father*s and *Hail Mary*s. There is more to it than briefly reviewing biblical scenes. The Blessed Mother also wants us, through our reflection, to enter with her *into* those scenes that we call "mysteries" and to *remain* in them through contemplation until they bring us closer to God and His Son. In so doing, we will share the concerns of the Immaculate Heart. We will occupy the same spiritual space as the Virgin Mary, whose interest and attention are always focused on God. She desires that our lives have the same focus.

The Rosary is the great prayer of ordinary Catholics. It brings remembrance of Scripture, words of offering and prayer for one's daily needs and the needs of our world, and a prophetic understanding of the world.

Remembrance of Scripture. Historically, the term *mystery* designates an event told in the Bible. When the citizens of medieval cities gathered on Corpus Christi Sunday to see the reenactment of scenes from the Bible, they called the plays "mysteries." They used this term because the meaning of any biblical scene goes beyond the mere surface of events. Sacred Scripture, as the revelation of the unseen God, opens the door to divine mysteries beyond human imagining. No matter how deep our understanding, we can only partially comprehend God's words and deeds. The realities of God, hidden beneath the surface story, remain mysterious to us because they are beyond our grasp. Hence the term *mystery*. But God has given us Scripture, through which He has revealed much of His truth. To enter into Scripture is to approach understanding of the mysteries of God. To reflect with the Church on the meaning of Christ's life, as seen from Mary's eyes, is to enter the holiest places open to man. And so we reflect on the mysteries with Mary, who participated in them.

Words of offering. We attach our reflections on the mysteries to the formal prayers of the Rosary. Then we offer these prayers to the Lord for our intentions. Hence the Rosary becomes an offering for our needs and those of the world. Though the Bible is ancient, the subject matter of Scripture often accords with some of the deepest needs of our culture. We are in desperate need of an end to abortion, for instance, and of a new respect for human life. I always offer the prayers of the Visitation for this intention. What scriptural scene more accords with this need than that of the Visitation? When the Blessed Virgin visited St. Elizabeth, the two women rejoiced that they had babies in their wombs. The scene became like an extended pro-life hymn. There was no question of an immoral "choice" for these two holy women. How relevant to our lives this is. The end of abortion and contraception is a natural intention for which to offer the prayers of the Visitation. And so on through the Rosary. Meditation on the mysteries will lead us to see much of their inner meaning, and much of how this meaning applies to our prayer life. Every child of Mary should reflect on the mysteries and decide what to pray for with each of them.

Prophetic understanding. When we do this, we will develop a scriptural, prophetic understanding of our world. The Second Vatican Council stressed that we ordinary Catholics have some share in Christ's ministry as prophet, priest, and king. We are priests because through Him we can offer acceptable sacrifices to

God. We are kings because He gives us self-rule through the Holy Spirit, and enables us to live by His law. We are prophets because through His revealed word and the teaching of the Church we understand the moral and spiritual meanings of our lives. With the Church's help, we know how to interpret the world around us. We speak prophetically when we stand up for what is right. Meditation on the mysteries of the Rosary helps us toward this goal. When people of faith contemplate the world in Gospel terms, their insights are blessed. The psalmist was right when he sang to God, "I have more understanding than all my teachers when Your decrees are my meditation" (Psalm 119:99).

The mysteries

The scenes selected by the Church to form the Rosary now number twenty. They are arranged under four headings: Joyful, Luminous, Sorrowful, and Glorious. Under each heading comes a reflection on five spiritual and scriptural subjects, or mysteries. In the following section, the Bible passage relating each mystery is quoted. After that comes a reflection on the meaning of the scene, followed by a suggested intention.

How should we use the biblical accounts? What should be the result of our Saturday reflection on the mysteries? Christian writers have always maintained that meditation on Scripture has great value. St. Ignatius of Loyola, for instance, wrote in his *Spiritual Exercises* about this value. He encouraged his followers, the first members of the Society of Jesus, to recreate in their minds the circumstances of the most important scenes in the life of Christ. A Jesuit on retreat was to shut out everything distracting. He was to make himself see in his mind the scriptural setting, spiritually enter that setting, and then proceed through a series of thought exercises.

Consider, for example, the wedding at Cana of Galilee, where Jesus worked the miracle of turning water into wine (John 2). St. Ignatius would have instructed the retreatant to think of the hall where the marriage took place; of the guests, the banquet, the music; of the joy of the bride and groom; of the entire festive scene. Then of the alarm when the wine ran out. The retreatant would especially picture the principal characters in the scene, Jesus and Mary. (Jesus is the focus of all the *Spiritual Exercises*.) Then, in wonder and awe at the presence of God, the retreatant would see the action and hear the words of Our Lord and His Mother: how she took the initiative in encouraging Him to work the miracle, how He reluctantly responded, how she stated the great rule of Christian life to the servants — "Do whatever He tells you" (John 2:5). And then, marvel of marvels, how the many gallons of plain water suddenly were water no longer, but fine wine. At this clear mental realization of the presence of God, the retreatant was encouraged to enter into a *conversation* with God or Mary. St. Ignatius called these conversations "colloquies." The words he told his Jesuits to use were often the words of the Rosary itself, the *Our Father* or the *Hail Mary*. Sometimes they were the great prayer *Anima Christi*. The first Jesuits used these prayers to converse with God or the Mother of God in the very scenes of Scripture. They were thus able to *participate* in the Scripture, to relive it, and to bring back from it a heightened understanding and spiritual solace. We can do the same thing.

Whether we do just what St. Ignatius prescribed or not, his spiritual exercise of conversing with God is a good example of how to enter into a reflection on Scripture. A First Saturday reflection on the mysteries of the Rosary should be undertaken in the same spirit. Don't hurry. Mentally enter the scriptural scene. Listen to God. (*Listening to God is more important than talking to Him.*) Ask Him to give you insight into the Scripture, and wisdom to carry from it into your daily life. May St. Ignatius and all saints help us:

>to enter deeply into the mysteries of the Blessed Virgin,
>to learn from the life of Christ what God wants us to learn,
>to enable us to live sanctified lives,
>to make reparation to the Immaculate Heart of Mary,
>and so to prepare us for an eternity in Christ's presence.

How to Use this Book in Saying the Rosary

Begin by making the sign of the cross and praying "In the name of the Father, the Son, and the Holy Spirit." Then say the *Apostles' Creed*:

> I believe in God, the Father Almighty, Creator of heaven and earth. And in Jesus Christ, His only Son, our Lord. Who was conceived by the power of the Holy Spirit, born of the Virgin Mary, suffered under Pontius Pilate, was crucified, died, and was buried. He descended into hell. On the third day He arose from the dead. He ascended into heaven and is seated at the right hand of God, the Father Almighty. Thence He shall come to judge the living and the dead. I believe in the Holy Spirit, the holy Catholic Church, the communion of saints, the forgiveness of sins, the resurrection of the body, and life everlasting. Amen.

Then say one *Our Father* and three *Hail Marys*. Offer the *Our Father* for the intentions of the pope and the health of the Church. Offer the *Hail Marys* for an increase of the theological virtues — faith, hope, and charity.

Then you're ready to begin with the mysteries:

Choose which set of mysteries — joyful, luminous, sorrowful, or glorious — you want to reflect on.

Read the first part about each mystery, usually called "the biblical scene," in the following discussion. If there is time, read and reflect on the rest of the section. Otherwise, come back to the appropriate section at your leisure, before or after you say the Rosary. Do this until you have finished the reflections. *The Rosary has been such an unmerited blessing in my life. It is my prayer that these reflections will lead you to your own fruitful thoughts on Jesus, Mary, and our salvation, and that your intimacy with Our Lord and His Mother may increase as a result. May God bless you in this way.*

Then go on to the prayers: one *Our Father*, ten *Hail Mary*s (a "decade"), and one *Glory be to the Father* for each mystery. Take your time if you can. Reflect on what the mystery means in itself, and in your life and in the world around you. Offer your prayers for some worthy intention.

After you finish five decades, either end with the concluding prayers or go on to another five decades.

At the end of your Rosary, say the concluding prayers. Some people alternate between the *Salve Regina* and some other Marian prayer such as the *Memorare*. In my private Rosary, I say the *Memorare* with the joyful, luminous, and sorrowful mysteries, and the *Salve Regina* with the glorious mysteries.

The Salve Regina:

> Hail Holy Queen, Mother of Mercy, our life, our sweetness, and our hope! To thee do we cry, poor banished children of Eve. To thee do we send up our sighs, mourning, and weeping in this valley of tears. Turn then, O most gracious Advocate, thine eyes of mercy toward us, and after this our exile, show us the blessed fruit of thy womb, Jesus. O clement, O loving, O sweet Virgin Mary.
> *Versicle*:   Pray for us, O holy Mother of God.
> *Response*:   That we may be made worthy of the promises of Christ.

The Memorare:

Remember, O most gracious Virgin Mary, that never was it known that anyone who fled to your protection, implored your help, or sought your intercession was left unaided. Inspired with this confidence, I fly to you, O Virgin of virgins, my Mother. To you I come, before you I stand, sinful and sorrowful. O Mother of the Word Incarnate, despise not my words, but in your mercy hear and answer me. Amen.

Versicle: Pray for us, O holy Mother of God.
Response: That we may be made worthy of the promises of Christ.

Optional final prayer:

O God, whose only begotten Son, by His life, death, and Resurrection, has purchased for us the rewards of eternal life, grant, we beseech Thee, that after meditating on these mysteries of the Most Holy Rosary of the Blessed Virgin Mary, we may imitate what they contain and obtain what they promise. Through the same Christ, our Lord. Amen.

The Joyful Mysteries

1. The Annunciation

The biblical scene. The scriptural account of the Annunciation is found in Luke 1:26-38:

> In the sixth month the angel Gabriel was sent from God to a city of Galilee named Nazareth, to a virgin betrothed to a man whose name was Joseph, of the house of David; and the virgin's name was Mary. And he came to her and said, "Hail, full of grace, the Lord is with you!" But she was greatly troubled at the saying, and considered in her mind what sort of greeting this might be. And the angel said to her, "Do not be afraid, Mary, for you have found favor with God. And behold, you will conceive in your womb and bear a son, and you shall call his name Jesus. He will be great, and will be called the Son of the Most High; and the Lord God will give to him the throne of his father David, and he will reign over the house of Jacob for ever; and of his kingdom there will be no end." And Mary said to the angel, "How can this be, since I have no husband?" And the angel said to her, "The Holy Spirit will come upon you, and the power of the Most High will overshadow you; therefore the child to be born will be called holy, the Son of God.

And behold, your kinswoman Elizabeth in her old age has also conceived a son; and this is the sixth month with her who was called barren. For with God nothing will be impossible." And Mary said, "Behold, I am the handmaid of the Lord; let it be done to me according to your word." And the angel departed from her.

We see parts of two wonderful prayers imbedded in this scriptural narrative: the *Hail Mary* and the *Angelus*. The archangel Gabriel greats Mary with words that later became the beginning of the *Hail Mary*: "Hail [Mary] full of grace, the Lord is with you." And the Blessed Virgin answers him with a verse that later became part of the *Angelus*: "Behold, I am the handmaid of the Lord; let it be done to me according to your word."

The *Hail Mary* is a simple but beautiful composite of Gospel passages on the Annunciation and the Visitation. In the next mystery, St. Elizabeth wonders at the great favor that God has shown Mary: "Blessed art thou among women, and blessed is the fruit of thy womb, Jesus." To Gabriel's words and Elizabeth's the Church later added our earnest request to the Mother of God, "Pray for us sinners now and at the hour of our death." This petition is based on the Church's understanding of Mary's privileged role in the communion of saints, which is in turn based on her role in salvation history as the Mother of the Savior. Mary is the pivotal human figure in the Incarnation, responsible for God's becoming man. She is later exalted for this role in her glorious Assumption into heaven. Now she is in a privileged place of access to the Holy Trinity, where she can "pray for us sinners now and at the hour of our death."

The *Angelus*, the other prayer that draws on this passage, is essentially a short reflection on how, with Mary's cooperation, God entered into His own creation in order to save it. Traditionally, the Church reminds herself of these great and humbling facts at six in the morning, noon, and six in the evening. A great custom.

Mary's role. The Annunciation by the angel to the Blessed Mother is the most important announcement ever made. But it also depends upon Mary's vital response. Upon Our Lady's free response hangs the salvation of the world. St. John writes that, when Mary said Yes, "the Word became flesh." God "became flesh" — was enfleshed, or incarnated — as a result of Mary's freely chosen agreement: "Let it be done to me according to your word."

God Himself took flesh from the Virgin Mary. When God became one of us, He miraculously began to form a human body in Mary's womb. He took upon Himself the blood and culture of her race. He also took upon Himself the whole composition of a man — and so became the brother of all human beings. For her part, Mary became the universal Mother of all whom her Son came to redeem. How significant is the Annunciation and its subject, the Incarnation? St. Cyril of Alexandria is worth quoting at length, for he was largely responsible for the Church's acceptance of "Mother of God" as Mary's title. Here is what he says about the Blessed Virgin's accomplishment in her cooperation with God:

> We salute you [Mary], for in your holy womb was confined Him who is beyond all limitation. Because of you the Holy Trinity is glorified and adored; the cross is called precious and is venerated throughout the world; the heavens exult; the angels and archangels make merry; demons are put to flight; the devil, that tempter, is thrust down from heaven; the fallen race of man is taken up on high; all creatures possessed by the madness of idolatry have attained knowledge of the truth; believers receive holy baptism; the oil

of gladness is poured out; the Church is established throughout the world; pagans are brought to repentance. (From a homily delivered at the Council of Ephesus, AD 431.)

No greater influence, no greater importance, could be imagined.

The Church teaches that we all have a vocation. We may think of Mary's free response to God's call as the expression of *her* vocation. It is no coincidence that her words also express the *universal vocation of man*. It is Mary's vocation to continue saying "Yes" to God throughout her life, and even beyond her earthly journey. This is also your vocation, and mine. The Rosary emphasizes Mary's calling. In all the scenes of the Rosary, we see her either clearly in the foreground or implied in the background, as she continues to accept whatever God sends to her. Sometimes this acceptance is very painful. She saw Jesus on the way to His crucifixion. She saw him hanging, nailed on the cross. <u>*Our* vocation is similar — to take up the cross and follow Jesus, no matter what happens, good or bad. This is what Mary did; this is what we must do</u>. Her vocation is acceptance of *God's* will, not assertion of her own.

But her accepting *fiat* is also joyful. Whether in pain or joy, the Blessed Virgin Mary obediently accepts the will of God and carries it out. In this, she is a supreme example to all of us, her children.

Intention. For what shall we offer this decade of the Rosary? Perhaps in thanksgiving for the Incarnation, which brought God into saving communion with mankind. Perhaps also for the gift of obedience and acceptance of God's will, in imitation of Mary. The gift of accepting God's will in all that we do, again in imitation of our Blessed Mother: that is a worthy intention. Perhaps

The Joyful Mysteries

also we should pray for discernment about our own vocation. Whatever we decide to pray for, let us offer this decade for our deepest needs. May God help us to discern how His Son and the Blessed Mother wish to bless us in these prayers, and may we offer ourselves on behalf of these Spirit-guided petitions. Amen.

8/5/2017

2. The Visitation

The biblical scene. Like the Annunciation, the story of the Visitation is recorded by St. Luke (1:39-56):

> In those days Mary arose and went with haste into the hill country, to a city of Judah, and she entered the house of Zechariah and greeted Elizabeth. And when Elizabeth heard the greeting of Mary, the babe leaped in her womb; and Elizabeth was filled with the Holy Spirit and she exclaimed with a loud cry, "Blessed are you among women, and blessed is the fruit of your womb! And why is this granted me, that the mother of my Lord should come to me? For behold, when the voice of your greeting came to my ears, the babe in my womb leaped for joy. And blessed is she who believed that there would be a fulfillment of what was spoken to her from the Lord."

And Mary said,
>> My soul magnifies the Lord,
>> and my spirit rejoices in God my Savior,
>> for He has regarded the low estate of His handmaiden.
>> For behold, henceforth all generations
>> will call me blessed;
>> for He who is mighty has done great things for me,
>> and holy is His name.
>> And His mercy is on those who fear Him
>> from generation to generation.
>> He has shown strength with His arm,
>> He has scattered the proud
>> in the imagination of their hearts,

The Joyful Mysteries

> He has put down the mighty from their thrones,
> and exalted those of low degree;
> He has filled the hungry with good things,
> and the rich He has sent empty away.
> He has helped His servant Israel,
> in remembrance of His mercy,
> as He spoke to our fathers,
> to Abraham and to his posterity for ever.

And Mary remained with her about three months, and returned to her home.

What are the essential elements of this wonderful scene? Many currents run together here. First, there is the surface narrative. In it, the Blessed Virgin hears of her cousin's probably miraculous pregnancy. Realizing that St. Elizabeth must be in need of help and female companionship, Mary goes into the "hill country" to visit her. Hence the term Visitation.

For her part, St. Elizabeth embodies the ideals of hospitality and friendship. She welcomes Mary's three-month visit and rejoices in her company. Not to mention the company of Mary's divine Son.

One element that is notably absent from this story is any complaint about childbearing. St. Elizabeth and the Blessed Mother are not at all modern feminists — women who deny real differences between the sexes, want to be exactly like men, and resent the maternal role of women. There is no hint in this biblical scene that children are a curse or a burden. *That* immoral outlook is part of our cultural creed. Nor is there any hint that the world is "overpopulated." The utterly false idea that there are too many human beings is an uncritically accepted modern dogma, taught in schools and churches and embodied in government policies around the world. No, St. Elizabeth and the Virgin Mary are overjoyed to have the privilege of being (as the Church puts it) co-creators with God. They understand — miraculous elements aside — that children are a very great blessing from God. These holy women know that the highest feminine calling — indeed, perhaps the highest human calling — is the vocation to motherhood. They know that the greatest privilege and responsibility is to bear children into the world and raise them in the service of their Creator. Every child is created in God's image. Every parent is called to raise children in whom God's image is radiant. Elizabeth and Mary know this, and they react to their calling as mothers with joy and gratitude.

In addition to the surface story of Mary's visit to Elizabeth, the Visitation is the story of a miraculous spiritual encounter. St. Elizabeth spells it out: "When the voice of your greeting came to my ears, the babe in my womb leaped for joy." St. John "meets" Jesus of Nazareth for the first time. When he does so, he leaps for joy. So St. Elizabeth is not the only one to recognize "the mother of my Lord." The unborn St. John responds to the divine presence in Mary's womb and, in doing so, acknowledges Mary's role in the Incarnation. It is as if St. John already knows Mary as the Mother of God — a title that took centuries to become Church teaching. Throughout the Visitation, as throughout the entire Infancy Narrative, there is an overwhelming sense of the divine presence: the Most High God enters intimately into the lives of His humblest servants.

Mary's role. A third major element in the story of the Visitation is Mary's poetic reflection on her role in the Incarnation. That reflection is called the *Magnificat*. This moving poem is, first, an expression of gratitude. The Blessed Virgin speaks from her soul — that is, from her inmost being — as she "magnifies the Lord." To magnify the Lord is to proclaim Him *magnus*, or great. "My soul speaks of the greatness of the Lord." Though nothing that any human being does can increase God's power or goodness, Mary's magnification of Him expresses the right response of an especially blessed creature to her Creator, in whom her spirit exults. We should all exclaim every day of our lives, "How great and good is God, the Lord, who created me, who sustains me, and who gives all good gifts to His faithful people."

In this great poem the Virgin is also reflecting on how God treats His humble servants. God is especially merciful to the poor in spirit, to the humble people who acknowledge His greatness and know that they are completely dependent upon Him. Human pride is a bar to God's grace. A haughty attitude is an impediment to one's membership in the Kingdom of God. High self-esteem divorced from the knowledge that one is nothing without God is a symptom of willful ignorance. In the *Magnificat*, the Blessed Virgin exults in the Lord because He lifts up the lowly who cannot lift themselves up. She rejoices in the singular blessing that God has bestowed upon her — the blessing that she is only beginning to understand — in asking her to bear His Son into the world.

Consider the paintings of the masters. In most of the wonderful artistic depictions of the Annunciation, Mary is shown as a girl at prayer, usually kneeling, with a prayer book at hand, while the archangel Gabriel addresses her and a shaft of light brings the Holy Spirit to her. We traditionally think of the Blessed Virgin as a young woman who was learned in the teachings and requirements of her Jewish faith. This concept is borne out by her insistence, in the Presentation, on obedience to the Law. (St. Joseph is her partner in this.) It is natural, then, that the praise for God in the *Magnificat* is expressed in echoes of the ancient Scriptures. Just as Hannah sang the praises of God when she bore Samuel in her womb, Mary sings His praises now. Just as Hannah reflected on how God lifts up His humble servants, Mary reflects on how God feeds the hungry and rejects the rich and self-sufficient. The *Magnificat* thus stands as a shining example of an ancient literary and spiritual tradition. The Church gratefully carries on this tradition by reciting the Virgin's song at Evening Prayer.

Intention. This wonderful story is pro-life at its core. It is relevant to our struggle for a culture of life. Here is a mystery of the Rosary that shows us a proper, grateful attitude toward God. The Visitation encourages us to receive children as a great gift from the Lord. It models the right response of a grateful daughter of the Heavenly Father when she is chosen to become a mother. It presents a pattern that needs to be held up before an errant culture of death, where the lives of unborn children are considered unimportant. Therefore one might offer this decade of the Rosary for an end to legal abortion throughout the world, and for the great conversion that such a change will represent.

3. The Birth of Christ in Bethlehem

The biblical scene. The fullest record of Christ's birth is in the Gospel of St. Luke:

> In those days a decree went out from Caesar Augustus that all the world should be enrolled. This was the first enrollment, when Quirinius was governor of Syria. And all went to be enrolled, each to his own city. And Joseph also went up from Galilee, from the city of Nazareth, to Judea, to the city of David, which is called Bethlehem, because he was of the house and lineage of David, to be enrolled with Mary, his betrothed, who was with child. And while they were there, the time came for her to be delivered. And she gave birth to her first-born son and wrapped him in swaddling clothes, and laid him in a manger, because there was no place for them in the inn (Luke 2:1-7).

Think of the meaning of Christmas. This great festival celebrates the birth of the Creator in His own creation. He who is light, wisdom, and order plunges into a disordered world, darkened by sin and strife. Our world. God, in short, becomes man. For nine months He is protected in the womb of the Virgin. Then, at the Nativity in Bethlehem, the world learns of His advent. Christmas celebrates a blessed step in the Epiphany, the making-known of God's plan of salvation. From the time of His conception in Mary's womb, the Lord has been flesh. But it is at His Nativity that He literally comes out to the world — first to the shepherds, then to the wise men, then to all the world. After His Incarnation at the Annunciation, after the Mother of

God had visited St. Elizabeth, the Savior was first presented to the human race as a newborn baby in the City of David. God's great act of redemption was becoming known. The course of world history was being radically reversed.

Jesus was born against a background of cosmic disaster. The catastrophe of the Fall had driven the first human beings from their garden home. The human race had labored in darkness for thousands of years. Human will was twisted. Separated from God, the best people groped toward their original goodness, but found that their own efforts were fruitless. Man was not dependent on his own talents, however, for God's promise of redemption gradually became evident. During Old Testament times, hope began to glow in prophecy. The understanding grew that a Messiah was coming. Faithful people yearned for His arrival. "O that out of Zion would come the salvation of Israel," the psalmist wrote (Psalm 14:7, New American Bible). The Anointed One for whom the faithful waited would create a new heaven and a new earth, and would reverse the catastrophic effects of sin. Just as the first Adam brought darkness and futility to human striving, the Second Adam would come as the Light of the World, the Dayspring from the East. That sunrise came at *Christmas* from the womb of a Virgin in a dark little stable on the edge of a small, isolated and unimportant town. God sends the greatest grace into the most unlikely places. As the poet Chaucer wrote, God can send His grace even into a little ox's stall.

Mary's role. As Christ is called the New Adam, Mary is called the New Eve. As the first Eve listened to the devil with disastrous consequences, the New Eve listens to God, and so brings to the human race the greatest possible blessing. Eve's son murdered his brother. Mary's Son — whose blood "speaks more eloquently than that of Abel" (Hebrews 12:24, New American Bible), speaks of redemption and reconciliation with the Father — redeems the original Adam and Eve and all their progeny. Indeed, He redeems the Virgin herself, who was chosen and divinely prepared to bear Him into the world. Sin had thrust the universe back into spiritual chaos. Mary's obedience restored the image of God in man. Mary is therefore the New Eve, Mother of all who find atonement with the Father in her Son's blood.

Until the Nativity, the Blessed Virgin and only a very select few had known about the coming of God as man. We may think of the Nativity of Jesus at Bethlehem as part of a series. That series began with the Annunciation, where there was only one human being present. Then, with the Visitation, a few more people learned of the monumental events that were occurring. But with the Nativity — announced as it was by something so visible as a bright star, and celebrated by a chorus of angels — the Incarnation became public. Mary, Joseph, even domestic animals witnessed the glorious birth of Jesus. The extremes of society, shepherds and kings, came to worship. As the circle of divine light grew, the manifestation — the Epiphany — of God on earth was proceeding, bringing joy and hope to a broken world. Mary, the ark of the New Covenant, brought all this to pass through her cooperation with God. She invites all of us, her children, into the circle.

Intention. All of our prayers should include thanksgiving to God for His great bounty to us. No blessing could be greater than the coming of Jesus to save the human race. So our Nativity prayers should be offered in gratitude for the Christ Child, whose saving mission was becoming known at His birth. Since our world is more and more hostile to public acknowledgment of God, we should also pray — and work — for the conversion of our culture to the truth of Christ. We should pray that He be born and reborn in the thoughts, words, and actions of everyone. And here or elsewhere, we should pray for everyone whose lives we have touched, especially those whom we have hurt or influenced for evil.

4. The Presentation of Jesus in the Temple

The biblical scene. The biblical account of the Presentation also comes from St. Luke 2:22-38:

> And when the time came for their purification according to the law of Moses, they brought him up to Jerusalem to present him to the Lord (as it is written in the law of the Lord, "Every male that opens the womb shall be called holy to the Lord") and to offer a sacrifice according to what is said in the law of the Lord, "a pair of turtledoves, or two young pigeons." Now there was a man in Jerusalem, whose name was Simeon, and this man was righteous and devout, looking for the consolation of Israel, and the Holy Spirit was upon him. And it had been revealed to him by the Holy Spirit that he should not see death before he had seen the Lord's Christ. And inspired by the Spirit he came into the temple; and when the parents brought in the child Jesus, to do for him according to the custom of the law, he took him up in his arms and blessed God and said,
> "Lord, now lettest thou thy servant depart in peace,
>   according to thy word;
> for mine eyes have seen thy salvation
> which thou hast prepared in the presence of all peoples,
>   a light for revelation to the Gentiles,
>   and for glory to thy people Israel."
> And his father and his mother marveled at what was said about him; and Simeon blessed them and said to Mary his mother,
> "Behold, this child is set for the fall and rising
>   of many in Israel,

> and for a sign that is spoken against
> (and a sword will pierce through your own soul too),
> that thoughts out of many hearts may be revealed."
>
> And there was a prophetess Anna, the daughter of Phanuel, of the tribe of Asher; she was of a great age, having lived with her husband seven years from her virginity, and as a widow till she was eighty-four. She did not depart from the temple, worshipping with fasting and prayer night and day. And coming up at that very hour she gave thanks to God, and spoke of him to all who were looking for the redemption of Jerusalem.

Some people interpret major characters and events in the Bible as "archetypes" — that is, as symbols of fundamental human experience common to all ages and times. As long as we remember that biblical events are historically true as well as symbolic, archetypal analysis may be good. It is not too far removed from, for instance, the commentaries of St. Augustine. Real archetypes are concrete representations of universal human elements. And in the Presentation is embodied one of these, a picture at the very center of human life. Here a young mother presents her Firstborn to His Father. That is a true archetype. Could any event more perfectly capture the warm heart of human existence? The scene has been the subject of many beautiful works of art. Small wonder, for it embodies the dearest experience of humanity.

This wonderful biblical scene gives a dramatic emphasis to the reality of God's Incarnation. One aspect of Christ's true humanity was His membership in the chosen people, Israel. We Christians sometimes think of Jesus as merely ending the Jewish religion, but that interpretation ignores the continuity of the Bible. Prophecies concerning the Messiah occur in the Jewish

Scriptures and not elsewhere. (The Latin poet Virgil may have had some prophetic insight about the virgin birth. So the Church Fathers thought.) The Gospel of St. Matthew and the Letter to the Hebrews are two New Testament books that strongly emphasize this continuity. St. Paul taught that rather than ending the Old Covenant, Jesus *fulfilled* it — a teaching that Jesus Himself voiced. The Lord said that He had come not "to abolish the law and the prophets" but "to fulfill them" (Matthew 5:17). So the New Covenant is the latter end of the Old Covenant. The two are organically joined. Jesus Christ is the true subject of the whole of Scripture, not just of the New Testament.

Mary's role. Far from rejecting the Law, Joseph and Mary religiously observe it. That is why they go to the trouble to present Jesus to the Father. Every firstborn, whether animal or human, we are told in the Old Testament, is to be given to God (Exodus 13: 2). So the Presentation is required by the Jewish Law. I emphasize this because I believe it is central to the meaning of this mystery, and central to the example we should take from it. If anything is to be done, let it be done according to God's Law. We live in the era of grace, inaugurated by the coming of Jesus. But grace *fulfils* the Law; it doesn't erase it. Too many of our contemporaries, even in the Church, think that *obedience* to God is no longer especially important, since Jesus has brought us the grace that transcends the Law. But Jesus Himself taught that the Law is eternal, and that observance of it, rightly understood, is necessary for salvation. Remember what He told the young man who came to Him and asked, "What good deed must I do to have eternal life?" Jesus answered, "Keep the commandments" (Matthew 19:16-17). Let us follow the Blessed Virgin in her obedience to the Law. In doing so, we do not deny the saving power of Christ's blood and of the sacraments; rather, we affirm them by following Christ's own commands. After all, the Law is part of nature itself as well as God's revelation. The natural law taught in Church Tradition says that all people are to honor God above all, and live in love and moral uprightness with their neighbors.

At the Temple, St. Simeon and St. Anna help us to focus on Mary and her Son. These two devoted old people receive and marvel at the Holy Presence. And because they are prompted by the Holy Spirit, they speak in praise and prophecy. Simeon and Anna are examples of a developing consciousness among the Jewish people that the Messiah's coming was imminent. The sense had grown that the Law was incomplete, or at least not fully understood, and that the principles of justice expressed in Exodus and Deuteronomy were lacking in something. Justice said that servants of God will prosper. But instead God's servants often suffered. The apparent conflict between God's promises and the realities that the Jews faced had often been noted. In many poignant psalms, for instance, the psalmists ask God to bring help to His suffering people. "How long," they reverently ask, "are You going to wait?" But the very fact that His people were suffering and downtrodden led to the conclusion that God's justice was not the object of an earthly, present promise, but of a promise to be fulfilled in the next world. This is the promise that Jesus fulfills. "My kingdom does not belong to this world," He teaches (John 18:36).

Simeon and Anna embody the longing of Israel for the coming of the Messiah. They are seekers for God. Though they have no very clear understanding of what the Lord is going to do, they recognize Him. Simeon, for whom God's promise has been fulfilled, expresses his readiness to die. He does so in the touching canticle that the Church still uses for Night Prayer. This holy man also recognizes the upheaval that the coming of the Messiah will cause. Further, he recognizes and foretells the pain that will come to the Blessed Virgin as she and her Son carry out their mission to the world. Simeon foretells Mary's future role.

Intention. In the Presentation we see how submission to

God's law is tied up with spiritual renewal. We seek the same renewal. We realize that the "new heaven and new earth" that Christ brings can be established only in accord with the will of the Father. And so a possible intention for this decade of the Rosary might be phrased: "For the true renewal of Holy Mother Church in fidelity to the teaching of Christ, and that we may do our part in that renewal." Amen.

The Joyful Mysteries

5. The Finding in the Temple

The biblical scene. Luke 2:41-52 reads:

> Now his parents went to Jerusalem every year at the feast of the Passover. And when he was twelve years old, they went up according to custom; and when the feast was ended, as they were returning, the boy Jesus stayed behind in Jerusalem. His parents did not know it, but supposing him to be in the company they went a day's journey, and they sought him among their kinsfolk and acquaintances; and when they did not find him, they returned to Jerusalem seeking him. After three days they found him in the temple, sitting among the teachers, listening to them and asking them questions; and all who heard him were amazed at his understanding and his answers. And when they saw him they were astonished; and his mother said to him, "Son, why have you treated us so? Behold, your father and I have been looking for you anxiously." And he said to them, "How is it that you sought me? Did you not know that I must be in my Father's house?" And they did not understand the saying which he spoke to them. And he went down with them and came to Nazareth, and was obedient to them; and his mother kept all these things in her heart. And Jesus increased in wisdom and in stature, and in favor with God and man.

It has been twelve years since the Presentation. The situation in the Finding is similar to that earlier scene. Mary and Joseph are still devout, still observing Jewish Law and even going beyond its demands. With their friends and relatives they make an annual pilgrimage to the Temple at Passover time.

The young Jesus is now a marvelous twelve-year-old. He is obedient to His Mother and His foster father both before and after this scene. All during the years of "silence," from the Presentation to the Finding, and then from the Finding to the Baptism in the Jordan, Jesus honors His Mother. He honors His foster father until Joseph's death. But that fact doesn't prevent Him from knowing at the age of twelve who His true Father is. Seeking to fulfill God's will — to foreshadow His ministry as King and embodiment of the Kingdom — He stays in His Father's house, the Temple, while Mary and Joseph travel back to Nazareth.

The *wisdom of the Incarnate Word* is the most important underlying theme in this mystery. In the Temple, Jesus' words amaze the learned teachers. Small wonder. Since He was incarnate before all time, and indeed outside of time; since He was the Wisdom by which the Father created the universe; since He was both the subject and author of the ancient books of wisdom; when He walked into the Temple, *Wisdom* walked in. Filled with the Holy Spirit, and exhibiting the gifts of the Spirit in all that He did, Jesus dazzled the wise men, the clergy, of the Temple.

In one of the most striking Old Testament messianic prophecies, Isaiah looks forward to the "rule of Immanuel," and prophesies that He will embody certain traits that came to be known as the gifts of the Holy Spirit:

> A shoot shall sprout from the stump of Jesse, and from his roots a bud shall blossom. The spirit of the Lord shall rest upon him; a spirit of wisdom and of understanding, a spirit of counsel and of strength, a spirit

of knowledge and of piety [Vulgate *pietatis*], and his delight shall be the fear of the Lord (Isaiah 11:1-3).

These traits are usually listed as wisdom, understanding, knowledge, counsel, courage, piety, and fear of the Lord. The young Jesus has the wisdom that leads to understanding and knowledge. He has the ability to give counsel. He already shows the fortitude, or courage, to carry out His mission. His piety toward His true Father is the whole motive of His life, and it is obvious that He reveres (or fears) God. These gifts underlay the answers that He gave the Temple elders. Wouldn't it be great to know what they asked Him and exactly what He said?

Mary's role. This joyful mystery points forward to the sorrowful mysteries. That is because here, as in the Presentation, Our Lady is confronted with the difficult parts of Christ's mission. These include a foretaste of suffering to come, the pain of temporary separation, and the beginning of a share in Christ's Passion. Finding Jesus is joyful, but losing Him in the first place is proof that a cross lies ahead. Having to *seek* Him is, after all, one of the Sorrows of the Virgin. What's more, our Blessed Mother's understanding seems to falter here. Here she continues learning the painful if mysterious lesson that St. Simeon had stated, that a sword would pierce her heart. She sees more and more that her role is to wait upon the Lord as His handmaid, to await the revelations to come, painful as they may be. Finding Jesus gave her joy. Recognizing that she didn't know what He was going to do — and learning to trust Him more completely — gave her pain. Without diminishing His respect for the Virgin, Jesus makes clear to her that love and obedience to the Father are the substance of His mission, and that Mary's vocation is to support Him, not to control Him. In effect, He says to her, "If you had more clearly remembered my origin and who my Father is, you would not have had to search for me. You would have known that I was in the Temple. I had to be about my Father's business." It would seem that learning more and more lessons in sacrifice is part of the Virgin's own cross. With her, let us lift our crosses and follow the Son of God. Let us share in His sacrifice that we may live eternally in His presence. Amen.

Intention. That we may seek and find Jesus as our Blessed Mother did; that we may receive the gifts of the Holy Spirit and, to the best of our ability, live by them; that the wisdom which God alone can bestow may characterize all our thoughts, words, and actions; that this wisdom may move our race toward the conversion that Jesus wishes. For these gifts, let us offer this decade of the Rosary.

The Luminous Mysteries

A New Part of the Rosary

Most Catholics are now aware that Pope John Paul II added five new mysteries to the Rosary. These he called the Mysteries of Light, or Luminous Mysteries.

In retrospect, what was surprising about the Holy Father's action was not that it occurred, but that it took so long. For centuries the Church had prayed the Rosary. It was always a great and wonderful prayer. The mysteries, its subject matter, had always been considered a "summary of Scripture." In the early days, especially for Catholics who didn't read, learning the biblical events celebrated in the Rosary was a sort of scriptural education. In an era when most people were illiterate, the Rosary was a great teaching tool for the Church. Through it the faithful came to know the most important events in the life of Christ, and to share them from the viewpoint of His Mother.

But there was always a gap in the subject matter, and that gap is what Pope John Paul filled. Before the Luminous Mysteries were added, the Rosary skipped from the Finding in the Temple to the Agony in the Garden. In other words, it omitted the whole active ministry of Christ, during which He

- instituted the sacraments of the Church or prepared for them,
- proclaimed the Reign of God, and
- demonstrated that He Himself was the embodiment of that reign.

Though many of us — I, for instance — were too dull-witted to notice, the Luminous Mysteries were *needed*.

And so we gladly embrace these mysteries now. We make them part of our daily contemplation. In so doing, we stand with Mary, the Mother of Light, and worship the Son of God — the Lamb whose light illumines heaven — as He gives His light to the world.

The Luminous Mysteries

1. Jesus' Baptism in the Jordan

The biblical scene. Here is St. Mark's account of Christ's baptism:

> It happened in those days that Jesus came from Nazareth of Galilee and was baptized in the Jordan by John. On coming up out of the water he saw the heavens being torn open and the Spirit, like a dove, descending upon him. And a voice came from the heavens, "You are my beloved Son; with you I am well pleased" (Mark 1:9-11, New American Bible).

This scene, perhaps more than any other, suggests the modern sense of the word *mystery*. It forces us to ask, Why was Jesus baptized? Here was the Lord of heaven and earth, born without original sin, guilty of no actual sin. Here was a Man who had no apparent need whatever of baptism because He was totally free of the blights that baptism erases. Far from needing forgiveness of sin, He is the one who forgives it. Far from needed admission into the Church, He is her founder and head. The baptism of St. John was a sign of repentance, but Jesus had nothing to repent. Baptism into the Church washes away sin, but Jesus had no sin. Born as He was of an immaculately conceived Mother, who herself bore no sin, Jesus was Himself immaculate. As the Son of God, He was sinless by nature. As the Son of Man, He was ready to put the devil and his temptations to flight.

Why then was He baptized? St. Matthew gives one reason that St. Mark omits, but it hardly dispels the mystery. In the Gospel of Matthew, Jesus tells John that He wants to be baptized because "it is fitting for us to fulfill all righteousness" (Matthew

3:15). But what does this mean? Turning to the Church Fathers, we learn that Christ's baptism was an act of righteous humility. These first great interpreters of the New Testament teach that Jesus was willing to act as an example for His Church even when He wasn't compelled to do so. This principle would seem to apply to all His actions. He taught, for instance, when He could have delegated the job of teaching completely to others. He worked miracles when He could have proved His divinity by empowering others to work them (this would, of course, have been a miracle). Even His death was not compelled, but was, as the Eucharistic Prayer says, "a death he freely accepted." I think the whole answer is related to Christ's humility. "Though He was in the form of God," as St. Paul writes, "He did not count equality with God a thing to be grasped" (Philippians 1:6). As Jesus Himself taught, He came "not to be served, but to serve, and to give His life as a ransom for many" (Matthew 20:28). So the Church Fathers teach that since Jesus put Himself at the service of mankind rather than on a royal throne, He humbly accepted the washing that was appropriate for fallen human beings. Thus He "fulfilled all righteousness."

But there is much more to the answer, and it is especially important for the Church. In being baptized, according to the Fathers, Jesus *cleansed the waters themselves*. He was not washed. In effect, He washed the water. This made water a fit sign of the great sacrament of Baptism. It made water potentially holy — a substance that could be used in the sacrament. Christ's baptism thus prepared a great gift for the Church.

Why water? Because the Lord needed a universally available, common element that could be made into a spiritual sign. Since Baptism is a symbolic burial, its sign is something in which one can be buried. (Sprinkling or pouring has constituted a symbolic burial since long before Christ, as the Greek playwright Sophocles illustrates in *Antigone*.) For the purpose, Jesus could have actually chosen dirt. It's appropriate for burial. But dirt is hardly a sign of *cleansing*, and cleansing from sin is the purpose of baptism. So dirt would seem to be a less appropriate sign. (It would also pose a serious problem for Christian communions that insist on total immersion in baptism.) In His baptism, Jesus therefore was choosing a sacramental sign — symbolic burial in water — in preparation for its use in the Church. In other words, He was instituting a sacrament.

This is the way the sacraments "work." They elevate common elements — water, bread, wine, oil, human hands, matrimonial consent — into signs of the presence of Jesus. But not signs only, for sacraments actually bring the graces they signify. In every one of them, Jesus Christ is personally present.

The baptism of Jesus also gives us a clear scriptural picture of the Holy Trinity: Jesus in the water, the Father above the heavens, and the Holy Spirit descending in the form of a dove. Like the Transfiguration — another of the Luminous Mysteries — Christ's Baptism emphasizes the fact that He is Lord and King and Son of God. To this the Father in heaven testifies, while the Holy Spirit brings divine empowerment to the Lord at the beginning of His ministry. The Transfiguration, however, doesn't openly depict the Holy Spirit. May we never forget the lesson of both scenes: that Jesus Christ is above Moses, Elijah, and John the Baptizer because He is the Son of God.

Mary's role. Mary's role is very much in the background here, not in the foreground. The scene that follows this one, however, as well as her presence in the Sorrowful and Glorious Mysteries, demonstrates that she was always a strong presence in the Lord's life. Indeed, there is no reason not to think that she may have witnessed Jesus' baptism. She surely would have been aware of St. John's preaching and baptizing, which must have formed part of the current conversation in Judea.

Was Mary ever baptized? We think of the Blessed Virgin as

later receiving some of the sacraments, especially the Eucharist and perhaps anointing. But just as baptism was unnecessary for Jesus, it was unnecessary for her, since she was conceived without sin. It's hard to imagine that she would have been baptized. Unless she did so, as Jesus did, to "fulfill all righteousness." If she was baptized, it was for exemplary purposes only. Mary is, after all, the greatest example of a Christian. Since baptism makes one a member of the Church, perhaps Our Lady submitted to this sacramental washing. But she didn't *need* it in order to obtain the saving grace of God, for she already had that in abundance.

Intention. Thus Jesus made water the sign and reality of His sacramental presence in Baptism. Three of the five Luminous Mysteries are devoted directly to the sacraments. As we offer these prayers, it is especially appropriate to meditate on the sacraments and to thank God for all of them. In this first mystery of light, we thank Him especially for the sacrament of Baptism, which erases our sin and makes us members of His Church.

2. The Wedding in Cana

The biblical scene. According to St. John's Gospel,

> On the third day there was a wedding in Cana in Galilee, and the mother of Jesus was there. Jesus and his disciples were also invited to the wedding. When the wine ran short, the mother of Jesus said to him, "They have no wine." And Jesus said to her, "Woman, how does your concern affect me? My hour has not yet come." His mother said to the servers, "Do whatever he tells you." Now there were six stone water jars there for Jewish ceremonial washings, each holding twenty to thirty gallons. Jesus told them, "Fill the jars with water." So they filled them to the brim. Then he told them, "Draw some out now and take it to the headwaiter." So they took it. And when the headwaiter tasted the water that had become wine, without knowing where it came from (although the waiters who had drawn the water knew), the headwaiter called the bridegroom and said to him, "Everyone serves good wine first, and then when people have drunk freely, an inferior one; but you have kept the good wine until now." Jesus did this as the beginning of his signs in Cana in Galilee and so revealed his glory, and his disciples began to believe in him (John 2:1-11).

St. John tells us that this marvelous event was "the beginning" of Christ's "signs," that is, miracles. He had already shown supernatural knowledge, as when He knew Nathanael's name without being told. But now, at the beginning of His public ministry, He transcends all previous acts. He uses Jewish ceremonial vessels to do so, and thereby repudiates the old ceremonies while demonstrating His divinity. St. John tells us that Jesus' miracles are intended to help us believe in Him.

In addition to its significance as the beginning of His ministry of miracles, and in addition to the fact that Mary prompts Jesus' show of "glory," this mystery includes two more very important meanings. First, in turning water into wine, the Lord prefigures the Eucharist. Water is really *changed* here; there is no suggestion that its change is an illusion or pretense — just as, for the faithful, there is no suggestion that wine isn't really changed on the altar during Mass. Turning a jug of ordinary water into wine involves genuine transubstantiation, just as turning wine into blood on the altar does. So this mystery is analogous to the later, and greater, mystery of the Mass. The first Luminous Mystery, the Baptism of Jesus, embodies a sacramental sign. So does the second.

Also, by attending a wedding, Jesus blesses the sacrament of Matrimony. He makes clear in His later teaching just what marriage is and means. The Lord teaches that marriage is permanent and exclusive. A truly married man and woman are "one flesh" that divorce cannot divide (cf. Matthew 19:6). In Holy Matrimony, a man and woman give themselves completely to each other. The gift includes the whole man and woman, including their fertility (unless, for no fault of their own, they are infertile). Therefore contraception and sterilization are excluded from Christian marriage.

Mary's role. In St. John's Gospel, the Blessed Virgin plays a major role at the beginning and toward the end of Christ's mission on earth. At the Crucifixion, in her role as Our Lady of Sorrows, she stands beneath the cross with St. John, while Jesus pronounces her the Mother of St. John and therefore of the Church. In that sad scene, He makes clear the filial duty and affection that Christians owe to His Mother. But here in the marriage at Cana, the Virgin might be called Our Lady of Hope. St. Joseph is evidently dead by now. Alone with her divine Son, Mary looks forward with hope and wonder to His Kingdom. Though she doesn't know the details of His ministry, she does know about Christ's miraculous birth and wondrous childhood. Consequently, she is able to point with confidence at the marvels about to be revealed. In so doing, she also states the vocation of all Christians: "Do whatever He tells you" (John 2:5). Christians, she says: follow the Light.

Significantly, this is also the vocational watchword that guided Our Lady throughout her life. The Rosary sums up Our Lady's role: In addition to the Joyful Mysteries of Christ's birth and childhood, Mary saw the dazzling light of the Luminous Mysteries; though she later saw many sorrows, she came to receive glory at the hands of God. In all her life, she stood by Jesus and did whatever He told her. That is why she is such a marvelous example for Christians. That is why she was assumed into heaven and crowned there. That is why she is the Mother of the redeemed.

Finally, this scene presents in capsule form the relation between Jesus and His Mother. Mary has the great honor — for which she has been prepared by her Immaculate Conception, and for which she has qualified by her cooperation with God — of starting the Lord off on His public ministry. Without intending any presumption, one might say that Jesus really doesn't *feel* like "going public" with His miracles and message yet. But He lets His Mother overrule His feelings. He claims at first that His unreadiness makes the dearth of wine irrelevant to Him: "How does your concern affect me? My hour is not yet come." But He allows the Blessed Virgin to make this life-changing decision, after which He is known as a miracle worker sent from God. Perhaps He calls her "Woman" not out of disrespect, but out of recognition of her role in salvation history. Mary is the new Eve, the new Woman, who comes to rectify what the original Eve had messed up. It is noteworthy that Jesus also calls Mary "Woman" when she stands at the foot of the cross. There, she clearly has a larger-than-individual role. She is being given the Church as her sons and daughters, and she is being given *to* the Church as our Queen and Mother. Could any other human being have pushed Jesus into changing water into wine? Would anyone else have even thought of it?

Intention. At Cana, Jesus graced a wedding by His presence, and in so doing blessed the sacrament of Matrimony and the man and woman who married. Later, in His own words and through the Church, He taught that a married couple, man and woman, is the foundation of the family, and that the family is the primary unit of society. Christian Matrimony is under attack today, however. Divorce, contraception, abortion, "trial marriage," adultery, fornication, masturbation, sexual sins of all sorts, homosexual couplings, pornography, hatred of children, selfishness — we are awash in degeneracy that threatens marriage. So we offer this decade of the Rosary to the Father for this intention: that the true and great sacrament of Matrimony will flourish in our Church and society; that Jesus and Mary will bless Matrimony and protect it against all attacks. We also pray that we will always take seriously Mary's rule of life: "Do whatever He tells you." May Mary, the Mother of God, help us all to live by this rule. Amen.

The Luminous Mysteries

3. The Proclamation of the Kingdom

The biblical scene. One might choose almost any event from Jesus' ministry to illustrate this mystery. For the whole mission of Jesus was to proclaim — and to bring — the Kingdom of God to His people. His miracles, His teaching, His prophecies, His gathering of disciples, His zeal for the Father, His bitter journey to Jerusalem and death — all of His public ministry was a luminous declaration that the Kingdom had indeed come on earth. Here is one striking biblical instance. It illustrates Jesus' claim to be the Messiah. It also teaches a related lesson on how to read the Old Testament. It was probably shocking to His audience in the synagogue.

> He came to Nazareth, where he had been brought up; and he went to the synagogue, as his custom was, on the sabbath day. And he stood up to read; and there was given to him the book of the prophet Isaiah. He opened the book and found the place where it was written,
> > The Spirit of the Lord is upon me
> > because he has anointed me
> > to preach good news to the poor.
> > He has sent me to proclaim release to the captives
> > and recovering of sight to the blind,
> > to set at liberty those who are oppressed,
> > to proclaim the acceptable year of the Lord.
>
> And he closed the book, and gave it back to the attendant, and sat down, and the eyes of all in the synagogue were fixed on him. And he began to say to them, "Today this scripture has been fulfilled in your hearing" (Luke 4:16-21).

Isn't it wonderful the way — from the Christian perspective — the whole Bible turns out to be about Jesus of Nazareth? The Old Testament as well as the New? Do we not marvel at the fact that God's Son, the eternal Word, turns out to have been the force of revelation behind the Law and the Prophets? Even a thousand years before His birth in Bethlehem? What a shock it must have been to the listeners in the synagogue as this obscure young prophet from Nazareth claimed that Isaiah was writing about *Him*. And: whatever was written about Him was written about the Kingdom. In fact, as the Church Fathers taught, the entire Old Testament points forward to the New. And most of the New Testament, especially the Gospels, is the record of the establishment of God's Kingdom. From the Gospel accounts of the Annunciation all the way to the Ascension of the Lord, and in the record of the early Church found in the Acts of the Apostles and the epistles, the establishment of God's Kingdom is revealed in ever-widening compass. This is a *mystery of light* indeed — the light of God's brighter and brighter revelation. And it has not stopped, for the Kingdom on earth is but a preview of that heavenly Kingdom where the Lamb is the Light of God (cf. Revelation 22:5). The Kingdom continues to receive new citizens.

That is why this mystery in a sense includes all the others. For the whole Rosary belongs to the revelation of the Kingdom. Therefore we reflect now especially on how Jesus revealed to the human race His own nature. How He revealed Himself as God. How He worked miracles to help people believe in Him. How He taught a new law of love. How He chose His apostles and commissioned them to spread the word — the light — about the mission of the Redeemer.

Jesus repeatedly announces the coming of the Kingdom in Himself: "If it is by the Spirit of God that I drive out demons, then the Kingdom of God has come upon you" (Matthew 12:28). How exciting it must have been to see this Cornerstone of the City

The Luminous Mysteries

of God in person. Foretold by the prophets, prefigured in ancient Israel, awaited by holy men and women such as St. Simeon and St. Anna at the Annunciation, and given birth by an immaculate Virgin, Jesus opens up to the world a growing understanding of God's great salvation. And afterward, He guides His Church to an ever-increasing knowledge of the height and depth of the Gospel. This is *light*, and it all belongs to the Kingdom. Let us look briefly at its spectrum: How did Jesus reveal His reign?

The Lord heals the sick. He feeds the hungry. He commands the weather to change. More importantly and powerfully from a spiritual point of view, He forgives sins, thus claiming authority over *spiritual* life and death as well as physical health. When He does these things, of course, He affirms that He is God. St. John says that this is the whole purpose of the miracles of Christ. John wrote his account of these "signs" "so that you may believe that Jesus is the Christ, the Son of God, and that believing this you may have life through His name" (John 20:31).

Without the King there is no Kingdom. The coming of Christ is itself the coming of the Kingdom. From all of the Gospel we learn that the King and the Kingdom are inseparable. It's not as if the King were a detachable part of some kind of spiritual government. It's that the Kingdom — the *reign* of Christ — is established by the *fact* of Christ. To belong to the Kingdom is to be *in* Christ.

And yet God lets us reject His reign if we choose. We have the fearful ability to belong to the Kingdom or to exile ourselves from it. How do we belong? By abiding in Christ's word, by which we "know the truth" and become free of error, sin, and death (cf. John 8:32). By becoming like little children who look to their heavenly Father with faith and trust. By being willing at all times to give up our own will and accept the will of God. By praying sincerely, as Jesus taught, "Thy Kingdom come" (Matthew 6:10). For it is only through our acceptance that God's reign will extend to our own hearts and minds. Do we think of this petition in the *Our Father* as being about other people more than ourselves? Not so. Though all the world be converted to Christ (would that it were true), if we don't seek to know and do His will we will remain outside His reign.

Finally, it is our vocation not only to abide in Christ's Kingdom, but to proclaim it to others. To tell the Good Story of how God has saved us in Christ is the *duty* of every Christian. This is true not only of bishops, priests, deacons, and religious brothers and sisters, but of everyone. The Second Vatican Council made the duty of the laity quite clear. It is the vocation of every Catholic to witness to the Faith — both by word and example. If our coworkers and neighbors don't know that the Church and her teachings are important to us — more important than any other allegiance — then we are not doing our job. We are not fulfilling our vocation. Judgment Day for us will reveal grave sins of omission. Souls that should have been saved may be lost because we were embarrassed to confess Christ before them. May God grant that every citizen of the Kingdom bear witness to God's salvation.

Mary's role. The Blessed Virgin continues in the background. We may be sure that she heard constantly of the public doings of her Son — how He preached and taught, how He worked miracles of healing and feeding, how He laid claim to His divine origin by forgiving sins. We may assume that Our Lady, like other women of Galilee, sometimes followed Jesus in His journeys. And that others in the crowds knew her as His Mother, and knew of her blessedness.

I have said that Mary's vocation was to live out the injunction that she uttered at Cana in Galilee: "Do whatever He tells you" (John 2:5). In doing this, she continues to fulfill the role that she described at the Annunciation: "Behold, I am the handmaid of the Lord; let it be to me according to your word" (Luke 1:38).

In this devout attention to her vocation, the Blessed Virgin is a model to us all — and a model citizen of the Kingdom of God. In her is no groping for high station, no self-promotion, no vanity. Mary is the epitome of wonder at the glory of God as she focuses entirely on her Son. She calls us to share this enthusiasm.

Intention. Therefore with this mystery we pray that — like Mary — we may enter ever more deeply into the liberating word of Christ. Thus we will remain in Him and His Kingdom. We pray that we may follow His precept by proclaiming God's word to all the world. For this is Christ's command and promise to us: "Go therefore and make disciples of all nations, baptizing them in the name of the Father and of the Son and of the Holy Spirit, teaching them to observe all that I have commanded you; and lo, I am with you always, to the close of the age" (Matthew 28: 18-20).

4. The Transfiguration

The biblical scene. Here is what St. Matthew says about how Jesus was transfigured; that is, how He was strangely changed in appearance:

> After six days Jesus took with him Peter and James and John his brother, and led them up a high mountain apart. And he was transfigured before them, and his face shone like the sun, and his garments became white as light. And behold, there appeared to them Moses and Elijah, talking with him. And Peter said to Jesus, "Lord, it is well that we are here; if you wish, I will make three booths here, one for you and one for Moses and one for Elijah." He was still speaking, when lo, a bright cloud overshadowed them, and a voice from the cloud said, "This is my beloved Son, with whom I am well pleased; listen to him." When the disciples heard this, they fell on their faces and were filled with awe. But Jesus came and touched them, saying, "Rise, and have no fear." And when they lifted up their eyes, they saw no one but Jesus only (Matthew 17:1-8).

This is a mysterious and wonderful scene. At first its meaning seems completely obscure; it's funny that a scene about light should be dark. But with meditation and divine help we can arrive at some understanding, if not complete comprehension.

Pope St. Leo the Great teaches that the Transfiguration had three lessons for the disciples who accompanied Jesus. First, it gave them a glimpse of the risen Christ, so that they would not feel defeated at the crucifixion. They were to understand that Jesus would triumph over death. Though their understanding was still far from complete, they were now equipped with the remedy for despair. Second, the Transfiguration includes the promise that the glory of resurrection is to belong to every faithful member of Christ's Church. He is the first to rise from the dead. When we rise, we also will be transformed. Not that we will be equal to Christ, but that we will share in His glory as far as we are able. Third, St. Leo teaches that the Law and the Prophets, represented by Moses and Elijah, bear witness to the truth of *Christ's* word. The Father speaks on Jesus' behalf: "Listen to Him." And the entire Old Testament — the Law and the Prophets — is brought to witness God's truth in Jesus. We also recognize that the voice of the Father elevates Jesus above Moses and Elijah. These two Old Testament leaders were superlative spokesmen for God. But Jesus is more: He is God's Son. Therefore we listen to Jesus, and see how His life and ministry confirm the truth of the ancient revelations. We see how Jesus brings all truth together in Himself. We look forward to the glory that His grace will bestow on us — our share of the Transfiguration.

Why did the disciples need to start understanding the Resurrection? Clearly enough, it was because they so far had no notion of what Jesus was really going to do. After the Transfiguration, they discuss among themselves the meaning of "rise from the dead" (cf. Mark 9:10). Their confusion is understandable. They are indeed confronted with something entirely new. For some centuries the Jewish prophets had taught the reality of *some* kind of resurrection. In numerous Old Testament passages a life after death is indicated. Sometimes this life is rather dull — an existence of gray wraithlike figures in a sort of underworld. But sometimes — as in Psalm 17 — the life after death is seen as a bright reward for those who have served God in this life. It is this latter idea that Jesus taught to His Church.

But the idea that they actually knew an individual who would rise from the dead was still quite foreign to the disciples.

Here was a man of flesh and blood, their Teacher. He was a Nazarene. He spoke Aramaic with a Galilean accent. He had a widowed Mother, Mary, whom He loved and protected. So how was this man, great leader though He was, going to bring about His Kingdom that was "not of this world"? What was He going to do? He had no army, He had no wealth, He had no respect from the leaders of His own people. What did He mean when He said that He must die and rise from the dead? When that death actually came — in spite of His teaching and promises — His defeat seemed absolute. And His followers dispersed in despair.

Their despair might have been much worse if they hadn't witnessed or heard about the Transfiguration. When St. Peter, on the night of the Crucifixion, fled in cowardice, he had plenty to think about. Perhaps he thought about how God the Father had changed Jesus on the mountain, so that He looked like Moses and Elijah (only brighter in appearance). Perhaps, after his initial despair, he recalled how the Father had glorified Jesus. And then when at the tomb he came to believe in the wonder of Christ's Resurrection, the whole meaning of "rise from the dead" became clear to him. Now he knew: Jesus rose from the dead with a glorified body. His followers are going to do the same. Indeed at the last day the whole human race is going to rise, some to eternal joy and some to eternal pain. St. Peter came to know Jesus as the "firstfruits of those who shall rise from the dead" (the words are St. Paul's, cf. 1 Corinthians 15:20, 23). The Transfiguration was a foretaste of this knowledge.

These are the first two of St. Leo's lessons. The third is the authority of Jesus over the Law and the Prophets. In a wonderful and unique scene, the Father bears dramatic witness to the identity of Jesus, and to the way in which He passes His mission on to His followers. Identity: Jesus of Nazareth is the Son of God. He is infinitely above the Law (Moses) and the Prophets (Elijah). Indeed, these pillars of the Old Covenant bore witness to Him in the Old Testament, though their message was frequently veiled. In the same utterance, the Father passes the mantle of authority, once the property of Moses and the Prophets, to His Son: "Listen to Him." As the fulfillment of the Law, Jesus brings new and more perfect teaching to the chosen people. In complementarity to the Old Covenant, and yet surpassing it in excellence, He bears supreme authority. "All authority," as St. Matthew teaches (28: 18). Jesus brings the era of grace, and asks His followers to preach the Gospel and so fulfill His mission. "Listen to Him."

This whole scene is preceded by Jesus' prophecy that some of His hearers would not die before they saw the Kingdom come in power. Then, "after six days," Jesus is transfigured. Surely Matthew and Mark intend the Transfiguration to be the event that shows Christ's coming "in power." The Transfiguration reveals that the Kingdom of God has come indeed, in the person of Christ. There is no need for us to look further for the fulfillment of Jesus' prophecy. We must prepare for His *next* coming "in power."

Mary's role. The Blessed Mother was assumed into heaven and crowned Queen of heaven and earth. She was given an immortal, glorified body. Because of her great faithfulness, Jesus called her to Himself. She is thus the prototype of the faithful Christian, to whom the Transfiguration promises glory and immortality. From her example we learn that humility and obedience are the way to this glory. We know that she truly deserved such a reward, just as surely as we know that we do not. By the grace of Jesus, however, we can arise to eternal life in Him and receive that "eternal weight of glory" about which St. Paul writes (2 Corinthians 4:17).

Intention. As we reflect on the Transfiguration and say the prayers of this decade, let us pray that we will always recognize Jesus as our Lord, the true Son of God. Let us beseech Him that we and all for whom we pray may someday receive the glory that the Transfiguration foretells for His faithful servants.

5. The Institution of the Holy Eucharist

The Institution of the Eucharist and its meaning in the lives of Catholics should be a lifelong subject of contemplation for us. Holy Communion should be the center of our lives, from which we draw strength and joy. In addition to the thoughts here, please see the "Reflections before the Blessed Sacrament" elsewhere in this book.

The biblical scene. St. Paul tells us the story of the Institution of the Mass, as he received it "from the Lord":

> I received from the Lord what I also delivered to you, that the Lord Jesus on the night when he was betrayed took bread, and when he had given thanks, he broke it, and said, "This is my body which is for you. Do this in remembrance of me." In the same way also the cup, after supper, saying, "This cup is the new covenant in my blood. Do this, as often as you drink it, in remembrance of me." For as often as you eat this bread and drink the cup, you proclaim the Lord's death until he comes (1 Corinthians 11:23-26).

The Mysteries of Light are wonderfully rich in sacramental teaching. None is more so than the mystery of the Institution. Like Christ's baptism in the Jordan, the Institution of the Eucharistic Sacrifice tells of Jesus' will to be with His Church. It speaks of how He took common things — bread, wine — and promised that in His Church they would be signs of His continued presence. But more than signs. For the Sacraments of the Church do not only symbolize Christ's presence, they actually *bring Him to us.* So in the Eucharist — both the joyful thanksgiving ritual in which bread and wine become the Body and Blood of Christ, and the consecrated elements themselves — we see the astonishing imprint of God's very heart, as He makes Himself present on our altars.

Can anyone understand this? One might ask why on earth the Incarnate God would do such a thing. Why *this* ceremony, in which He promises to become food and drink? What did God intend for us when He commanded us to eat His Flesh and drink His Blood, and so take divinity into ourselves? He divinized the human race by becoming one of us. By rising from the dead and ascending to His Father, He lifted flesh into heaven. Does His Institution of the Eucharist before His Passion prepare and enable us to rise and ascend in His name? Is that why the Risen One wants to be food? The answers are mysterious, and worth a lifetime of contemplation. Meanwhile, we must realize that the impetus for the Holy Mass was not "on earth" but "from heaven." And then we must continually remind ourselves of the joy and gravity of worshiping God in the Mass as we offer the Son to the Father, and ourselves with the Son. A mere human mind could never have imagined the Eucharist, and we can't fathom it. Nevertheless, we must enter wholeheartedly into it, for God *chose* the way of bread and wine to stay with His Church, and through it to point the way to divine splendors beyond our imagining.

The consecrated bread and wine on the altar are a sign that Jesus is there. On the first Holy Thursday, at the Institution of the Holy Mass, the Lord made bread a sign of His Body. He made wine a sign of His Blood. Whenever a duly ordained priest celebrates the Eucharist, he once again elevates these simple components of human life, bread and wine, to signs of Christ's Body and Blood.

But as in all the sacraments, the sign — though necessary — is only part of the reality. A sign is only a sign. It wouldn't be a sign if it didn't point to something important and real. The signs of bread and wine therefore not only represent Christ's Body and Blood. They actually *become* His Body and Blood, while retaining their surface features. After the consecration, the actual "breadness" of the bread is gone, replaced by the Body of the Savior. But the appearance of bread remains. The "wineness" of the wine — its substance — has been changed into Christ's Blood, though the accidental or surface features of wine — its color, alcohol content, taste — remain. The signs remain, the substance is changed.

So the bread and wine are both signs and means of Christ's presence. They say that He is on the altar, and they actually are His Body given up and His Blood poured out for us.

What is the essential difference between the Eucharist and the other sacraments? After all, they all include signs — oil, water, the laying-on of hands, the marriage promises — that actually make Christ present. The difference is this: The Eucharist is more profoundly connected to the pivotal act by which God brings salvation to the human race. That is, the Eucharist is directly founded on the sacrifice of the Lamb of God. Toward this sacrifice the other sacraments are oriented. The historical event, the narrative content, of the First Eucharist is the saving sacrifice of Jesus embodied in that bread and wine that He held out to His apostles in the upper room.

All the sacraments are vehicles of grace embodied in signs and actions of Christ's followers. But only one has such a distinct scriptural origin: the Eucharist. The origins of the marriage vows are hidden in the obscuring folds of time. The beginnings of anointing and baptizing are unknown. (Where did St. John the Baptizer learn about baptism? Was anointing not already ancient when Samuel anointed David?) When St. Paul mentions the laying-on of hands to St. Timothy, the practice is already established. We don't know where these signs, which Jesus uses in His

Church, came from. But we are very clear about the beginning of the Eucharist.

By the time St. Paul wrote to the Corinthians about the institution of the Mass, the story was part of Sacred Tradition. "I received from the Lord what I also handed on to you." Like all of Scripture, St. Paul's written account is drawn from the Spirit-guided Tradition, which preceded the Scriptures and even guided the Church in her judgment of what writings belong to the New Testament. In its context as the immediate introduction to the suffering, death, and Resurrection of Christ, the account of the Institution tells us the purpose of the Mass: To bring the saving power of Christ's sacrifice to all His faithful servants so that they may share in the victory of His resurrection. This is why, in both story and reality, sign and substance, Jesus has made Himself present in His Church throughout her history — so that He may *save* her. He comes to us now in this most intimate self-sacrifice. He becomes our food. We become His Body. His Blood flows in our veins, and enables us to live the life of grace.

Mary's role. In Mary's womb was formed the physical Body of Christ, which is present in the Sacrifice of the Altar in body, blood, soul, and divinity. Mary is the Mother of God. The Eucharistic elements are God. Therefore Mary is the Mother of the Eucharist. She is the first member of the redeemed Body of Christ and the first citizen of heaven, as she was the first influence on the Child Jesus. As He obeyed her on earth, He honored her by calling her to Himself at the end of her earthly life. When, after the Ascension of Christ into heaven, the early Church lived its eucharistic life, Mary took part in that life. Though far above the apostles, she received from them the Bread of Angels. Jesus thus prepared her for the miraculous change that occurred at the Assumption. Though the Blessed Virgin was not present at the Institution of the Eucharist — only potential priests were there — she was the foremost earthly preparer of the sacred feast, and its first and most holy beneficiary. We owe her gratitude and praise. We emulate her. We seek to follow her to an eternal reward.

Intention. May we truly live the eucharistic life. May the Eucharist become and remain the center of our lives. Through us, may it become the center of the lives of all to whom our lives and prayers pertain, for whom we now pray. Through the Holy Sacrifice of the Mass may all "men of good will" come to atonement with the Almighty Father, and to an eternity of light and peace in the presence of His Son. Amen.

The Sorrowful Mysteries

1. The Agony in the Garden

The biblical scene. Here is what St. Matthew says about the Agony:

> Jesus went with them to a place called Gethsemane, and he said to his disciples, "Sit here, while I go yonder and pray." And taking with him Peter and the two sons of Zebedee, he began to be sorrowful and troubled. Then he said to them, "My soul is very sorrowful, even to death; remain here, and watch with me." And going a little farther he fell on his face and prayed, "My Father, if it be possible, let this cup pass from me; nevertheless, not as I will, but as thou wilt." And he came to the disciples and found them sleeping; and he said to Peter, "So, could you not watch with me one hour? Watch and pray that you may not enter into temptation; the spirit indeed is willing, but the flesh is weak." Again, for the second time, he went away and prayed, "My Father, if this cannot pass unless I drink it, thy will be done." And again he came and found them sleeping, for their eyes were heavy. So, leaving them again, he went away and prayed for the third time, saying the same words. Then he came to the disciples and said to them, "Are you still sleeping and

taking your rest? Behold, the hour is at hand, and the Son of man is betrayed into the hands of sinners. Rise, let us be going; see, my betrayer is at hand" (Matthew 26:36-46).

Saint Luke adds that while Jesus was in the garden, "there appeared to him an angel from heaven, strengthening him. And being in an agony he prayed more earnestly; and his sweat became like great drops of blood falling down upon the ground" (Luke 22:43-44).

In this heart-rending scene the humanity of Jesus is on full display. True, He was fully divine. But He was also fully human. His divine mind gave Him knowledge of the great suffering that His mission entailed. It even gave Him a foresight of the victory that would come on Easter morning. But that knowledge could not wipe out the dread of pain and humiliation. Pain is an all-too-reliable marker of the human condition. Even Our Lord was not immune to the foreboding shudder with which the impending crucifixion shook Him.

Many people have said that Jesus' spiritual agony in Gethsemane was more painful than His actual physical suffering the next day. That is, however, something that we cannot know. What we do know is that His suffering in the garden was so extreme that it was the first chapter of His Passion. The Agony, even without the lash and the nails, pushed the limits of human capability. How many people do we know who have sweated blood because of the intensity of their internal suffering? Our Lord did. That kind of emotional and spiritual pain is simply beyond the limits of most human experience.

Behind the Agony lay — first — Christ's sure knowledge that great physical pain lay ahead. But His prescience of torture was not all. Look at the other elements of His pain. He was also deserted, at least in spirit, by His disciples. In a physical torpor

The Sorrowful Mysteries

that foreshadows his denial of Christ, St. Peter sleeps. And sleeps. He and the other disciples, even those closest to the Lord, can't rouse themselves to keep Him company, or even to keep watch. Jesus Himself notes that His betrayer is approaching — that knowledge having escaped His sleepy apostles. Surely loneliness — the knowledge that He was essentially suffering alone, without strength from His companions — was a part of His misery. Why else would He ask them to watch with Him?

And so He prays, a solitary man in agony, while sweating blood at the foreknowledge of His torment. He pleads that He might be spared the cup of pain and sorrow — the trial, the torture, the ridicule, the humiliation, the sheer overwhelming physical pain. But it is the Father's will, to which the Son dutifully and obediently submits, that Jesus go through all the scenes of His Passion. The Father says "No" to the Son. The Son must drink the bitter cup.

Other dark currents flow through Gethsemane. Surely — again humanly speaking — a sense of failure oppressed the Lord. He had come, He said, to redeem the House of Israel, but most of the Israelites had rejected Him. So He had in a sense failed in His purpose. He had acknowledged the great pain that this rejection brought. In an apostrophe to Jerusalem, He lamented that the city had refused to follow Him (Matthew 23:37). Perhaps the rejection of Jesus by the Jews was the Father's way of extending Christ's salvation to the Gentiles, to the whole world. Some modern writers think that if Jesus had been completely accepted by the Israelites, His followers would have been regarded as a mere branch of Judaism. Much of the appeal to the Gentiles might have been lost. It would seem that the Jews' rejection of Christ was part of the divine plan to establish a Kingdom for the whole human race. It was also a part of the sorrow of Gethsemane.

Mary's role. Where is Mary? At home, hearing the rumblings of judicial murder from the streets? With friends who are remarking on how Mary's Son entered Jerusalem triumphantly just four days previously, and now is the object of a military search led by the traitor Judas? Is it possible that Mary was unaware of the danger in which Jesus stood? Let us remember the great agony that the Lord endured so as to fulfill His mission as the Son of God. Let us also remember the horrible foreboding that the Blessed Virgin felt when she perceived the gathering threat to her Son. Let us stay close to the Immaculate Heart of our Blessed Mother, who, in these mysteries, is Our Lady of Sorrows.

Intention. When we are filled with foreboding; when we are hurt by the desertion of friends; when we face the suffering of disease, bereavement, loneliness, old age, or any other pain to which humanity is subject — let us remember Jesus in the Garden of Gethsemane. Our communion with Him in this garden of pain will sanctify our suffering. He will recognize in us the companions who do *not* sleep, and He will make of our suffering an offering to the Father. Lord Jesus, may we join you in your Agony. As your suffering was a holy sacrifice to the Father, lift us up to the heavenly throne and make of us an everlasting offering. Amen.

2. The Scourging at the Pillar

The biblical scene. St. Matthew's account of the Scourging:

> When Pilate saw that he was gaining nothing, but rather that a riot was beginning, he took water and washed his hands before the crowd, saying, "I am innocent of this righteous man's blood; see to it yourselves." And all the people answered, "His blood be on us and on our children!" Then he released for them Barabbas, and having scourged Jesus, delivered him to be crucified (Matthew 27:24-26).

The Gospel writers almost omit the Flagellation or Scourging of the Lord. In our version it is grammatically reduced to a transitional or insignificant detail, set off by commas. But it is more important than it would seem, partly because of its position in the mysteries of the Rosary. Over the centuries Christianity has paid enough attention to the Scourging that it has become a major part of the Passion. Realistically speaking — from a human point of view — to be brutally beaten for no offense at all must be very important indeed, though it pales by comparison with the Crucifixion.

To Pilate the Scourging was certainly subordinate. It seems like a mere afterthought — something he did just in passing. But the big question is: Why did he do it? It wasn't the custom for every condemned prisoner to be scourged before crucifixion. So it seems that Jesus was singled out for special punishment.

Some facts are obvious. The Scourging added to Our Lord's pain. As part of the Gospel story, it formed a sort of introduction to the climactic agony of the cross. It made the Via Crucis so much more painful, for the Lord's garments would have stuck to the wounds made by the whip; when His robe was removed, the skin would have come off with it.

But there are less obvious and more spiritual facts involved. Of these, above all, the Scourging seems to be an emblem of God's great humility. He had chosen not only to become a member of the human race — and therefore "most poor" — but to accept the treatment of a slave. For whipping is the lot of slaves and criminals, not of free and innocent men. One expects that a slave caught in thievery, or a seaman who insults an officer, would be scourged. It seems that Jesus' Passion includes punishments for the gamut of crimes, from insubordination to conspiracy.

Jesus predicted the Scourging and walked toward it with courageous acceptance. According to St. Mark,

> They were on the road, going up to Jerusalem, and Jesus was walking ahead of them; and they were amazed, and those who followed were afraid. And taking the twelve again, he began to tell them what was to happen to him, saying, "Behold, we are going up to Jerusalem; and the Son of Man will be delivered to the chief priests and the scribes, and they will condemn him to death, and deliver him to the Gentiles; and they will mock him, and spit upon him, and scourge him, and kill him; and after three days he will rise" (Mark 10:32-34).

Here the evangelist teaches that the Messiah knew in advance the main elements of His Passion. Just contemplating these horrors scares His followers — who follow Him anyway, knowing what awaits in Jerusalem. Notably, the Lord also foresees His Resurrection. But the foreknowledge of His victory over death cannot erase the apprehension of suffering from His human mind. Though suffering cannot be weighed, we believe that no one has ever suffered more. Indeed, the Lord's pains of body and mind were a plenum of human misery.

I think that the heart of the meaning of the Scourging is that Jesus completely accepted the mission that the Father gave Him. That mission included being treated like a slave. Because Jesus accepted His vocation in its entirety, He refused to consider Himself equal to the Father and accepted all of the humiliation that led to the cross (cf. Philippians 2:8). His calling led to His being treated with no dignity at all — as if He had no worth. In this sense the Scourging is another of the great paradoxes of our redemption: that the Creator of the universe, who gave it form and meaning and who holds it in being, should be treated as an outcast on earth and ground under the foot of soldiers. How great is God's love! How great is His condescension toward a race with hardened and erring hearts!

What picture does the Scourging present? Not that of a man standing upright, His arms stretched around a column. Though this is the customary image — and though the Scourging has received a vividly different cinematic representation in Mel Gibson's movie *The Passion of the Christ* — the Roman practice was actually to chain the victim's hands to the *top* of a short pillar so low that he had to bend down sharply. Then the torturer could bring the whip down with all his might. Gravity aided the scourger's muscles to produce a stroke that could tear away skin and cut the tissue underneath.

Mary's role. Our Blessed Mother is still in the background. We think of her as hearing reports of the treatment of Jesus, perhaps even as looking on from a distance. In no way would she have been admitted to the kangaroo court that tried and convicted, then scourged, her Son. But what pain must have come to her. What a sword must have pierced her heart (as St. Simeon predicted at the Presentation). How appalled she must have been to see her Son, who had changed water into wine, who had spoken with divine illumination in the presence of the elders of Jerusalem, who had miraculously fed multitudes, who had inspired the poor and outcast with divine hope — how appalled she must have been to see Him whipped like a slave. How hard it was for her to accept her vocation in this scene; to say as the Passion of Christ proceeds, "Be it done unto me according to your word." May we all follow her example as she humbly submits to God's will.

Intention. Lord Jesus Christ, Paschal Victim, sacrificial Lamb, you allowed yourself to be crushed in body and soul that you might become a perfect offering to the Father, in atonement for the sins of the world. We beg you to grant us the grace to accept the consequences of following you — even when this vocation brings us pain and abuse — that we may become in you an acceptable offering to the Father. For we know that by your stripes we are healed. Amen.

The Sorrowful Mysteries

3. The Crowning with Thorns

The biblical scene. St. Matthew writes that immediately after the Scourging,

> the soldiers of the governor took Jesus into the praetorium, and they gathered the whole battalion before him. And they stripped him and put a scarlet robe upon him, and plaiting a crown of thorns they put it on his head, and put a reed in his right hand. And kneeling before him they mocked him, saying, "Hail, King of the Jews!" And they spat upon him, and took the reed and struck him on the head. And when they had mocked him, they stripped him of the robe, and put his own clothes on him, and led him away to crucify him (Matthew 27:27-31).

According to St. John, after Jesus is crowned with thorns and robed in purple, Pilate presents him to the crowd:

> Pilate went out again, and said to them, "Behold, I am bringing him out to you, that you may know that I find no crime in him." So Jesus came out, wearing the crown of thorns and the purple robe. Pilate said to them, "Here is the man!" When the chief priests and the officers saw him, they cried out, "Crucify him, crucify him!" (John 19:4-6).

Then, after further questioning of Jesus inside the praetorium, Pilate took Jesus out again and sat down on the judgment seat.

He said to the Jews, "Here is your King!" They cried out, "Away with him, away with him, crucify him!" Pilate said to them, "Shall I crucify your King?" The chief priests answered, "We have no King but Caesar" (John 19:14-15).

We annually celebrate the Solemnity of Christ the King. Fittingly, we end the year with this great feast, before beginning on the following Sunday to observe the Advent countdown to Christmas. The universe will end as the Church year ends: with Jesus triumphant, reigning as King of Kings forever.

I think that most modern people have little sense of the meaning of kingship. This is true even in countries that have monarchs, for the features of a contemporary royal family are largely ceremonial and decorative. The old ideas of kingship are lost. And even if this weren't true, we would have to meditate on what the New Testament says about Jesus in order to understand *His* kingship, for He is a strange king indeed — a totally benevolent, completely self-sacrificing, yet all-powerful Being. There is no other king like this one.

How do the readings for the solemnity of Christ the King present the Lord? What kind of king do they depict? First, He is a shepherd. In biblical tradition, the shepherd's first concern is the welfare of the sheep. He guides them, protects them against predators, shelters them against the night, feeds them in green pastures beside quiet waters (Psalm 23), heals the sick, and seeks out the lost to return them to the flock. Ever since the shepherd-king, David, was anointed by Samuel, the Jewish people had known that the Messiah would be a shepherd. In His self-offering for His flock, Jesus, the Son of David, fulfils the role completely.

Second, the Scripture gives us the image of an all-powerful Being to whom even death is subject. A King indeed. Nations and peoples, principalities and earthly kingdoms, are all subject to His rule — although many people, both the affluent and comfortable and the poor and miserable, often refuse His authority. In the final scene of history, when the record of things said and done on earth is finished and sealed, death will die. God will wipe away all the tears of His faithful (cf. Revelation 7:17), who will shine like the stars forever (cf. Daniel 12:3). And death will have no more dominion.

But this is only half of the final division, and it brings us to the third aspect of Christ's kingship: Jesus the King is also the High Judge. He is going to judge every human being. By what standard? Specifically, by the standard of charity, the *caritas Dei*, the love that partakes of God Himself. If we do not have this love in us, we will exclude ourselves from God's presence forever. At the Judgment, those who in their earthly lives saw Christ in other people, especially the poor and afflicted, and served Him in them will enter into eternal life. The others, who ignored or persecuted Him in the needy — who lived for themselves and gave little thought to the needs of others — will be banished to hell forever (see Matthew 25:31-46). Then Jesus the Lamb will be all in all for the saved. Then all things will be made new for those who love the Lord (cf. Revelation 21:5).

Why is this? Why should charity, or love, be the standard of God's judgment? Why is the application of *this* standard the King's practice? Simply because it is through love and self-giving that we share in God's nature. Thus we conform ourselves to the cross. Through self-sacrifice we come to resemble the Christ. It is the Father's *self-gift* by which the universe was created in the beginning. The Father's loving affirmation of what He has made is what keeps all creatures in being. The "laws of nature" are nothing else than God's continuing affirmation of a world that He created and pronounced "very good" (Genesis 1:31). This is the reason that Jesus tells us to love God above all else: because God is love itself, and unless we share that love we are unlike God and cannot love our fellow man. Unless, like God, we overflow with goodness toward others and not merely with a will to serve and esteem ourselves, we cannot sufficiently resemble Jesus. And if we fail in this, we will simply not fit in with the society of heaven.

Strangely enough, the human race has reacted to these ideas with ridicule or disbelief. The most striking feature of the Crowning with Thorns is its mockery. Though He is the King of heaven, the only crown that Jesus ever received during His life on earth was this plaited garland of thorns, designed to produce great pain while parodying the shape of a true crown. The genuine King of the Jews, the true King of Kings, the Lord who made heaven and earth, is thus crowned with a fake crown. His tormentors bow to Him in fake obeisance. They hail Him with fake cheers. They give Him a fake scepter. In one of the most dramatically ironic scenes of human history, they offer false praise and real pain to the true King.

The chief priests' claim that "We have no King but Caesar" is not only treasonous against Israel and the God of Israel. It is also a lie, which they told to ingratiate themselves with the Roman officials. For they would gladly acknowledge another king if he would make them independent of Rome and restore the glory of David's kingdom. How terrible it is that they don't realize they are in the presence of the New David. How little they understand their own Scriptures. For they don't realize that the messianic King foretold by the prophets is to be like Jesus, to reign by service and sacrifice, not by force of arms and earthly grandeur. Their idea of kingship is too small. So they don't know the true King.

Mary's role. About the Blessed Virgin's role in the Crowning with Thorns: **(1)** Jesus reigns truly and supremely in her heart, and **(2)** she suffered great pain when she saw His kingship mocked. The Church's teaching about Mary grew out of her teaching about Christ. Accordingly, the magisterium has always emphasized the Blessed Virgin's position as "Handmaid" of the Lord. Our knowledge of Christ as God, for instance, led to our understanding that Mary is the Mother of God. That title led then to the Church's meditation on what such a maternal role must be like. All the way, the focus is on the God who became Man through Mary. Mary is the lens, the focus, the clarification, of the Lord. Historically, she is the channel through which He entered the human scene. When she sees Him in pain from that cruel crown, she mourns; but she also continues to enthrone Him in her heart. When she sees His true kingship mocked, she wonders how His reign will triumph; but she looks ahead with hope to that victory. Let us, with our Blessed Mother, focus on Christ's kingship, remember the mockery His love received, and invite Jesus to reign in our lives.

Intention. When we think that we deserve better treatment than we are getting, we should remember the Crowning with Thorns. When we think we should be honored, we should call to mind the crown that Jesus wore. When we are treated with genuine unfairness, we should reflect on the fact that this treatment puts us in Jesus' company. Do you sometimes have hurt feelings because you think you deserve praise or pay that you have been denied? St. Peter says that we are healed by Jesus' wounds. We are also healed of our wounded pride and self-pity by wearing the crown that He wore. May Christ grant that we wear *whatever* crown He sends us with humility, joy, and hope. For this let us offer this decade of the Rosary.

4. The Carrying of the Cross

The biblical scene. St. John's is the only Gospel account of Jesus' carrying His own cross: "They took Jesus, and he went out, bearing His own cross, to the place called the place of a skull, which is called in Hebrew Golgotha" (John 19:17). The other evangelists mention only Simon of Cyrene as the bearer of the cross. St. Mark says, "They compelled a passerby, Simon of Cyrene, who was coming in from the country, the father of Alexander and Rufus, to carry his cross. And they brought him to the place called Golgotha (which means the place of a skull)" (Mark 15:21-22). We need not worry about a contradiction here. The eyewitness accounts are complementary. Evidently Jesus began carrying the cross and then Simon shared the load.

All of the elements of the Passion share a striking characteristic: the injuries they cause are also insults. That crown of thorns was designed for both ridicule and pain. The Crucifixion, culmination of the Passion, lifted the Victim up to jeers while He died an excruciating death. Even the Agony in the Garden included the insult of loneliness and foreboding, just a few days after Jesus' triumphant entry into Jerusalem. We have seen the insult in the Scourging, which epitomizes the punishment of a slave.

And then the Carrying of the Cross: imagine being forced to carry the rope to your own hanging, or to bring the rocks to your own stoning. Jesus, exhausted and severely wounded, convicted of vague crimes on the testimony of false witnesses, known even by Pontius Pilate to be innocent, was sentenced to death and forced to carry the heavy crossbeam on which He was to be nailed. On the Way of the Cross He fell repeatedly under the weight, which pressed down on His mangled back.

It is small wonder that the cross became the major identifying mark of Christians. It was already the salient feature of Roman executions. Then, combined with Jesus' innocence and with His disciples' faith that He had risen from the dead, the cross gained great symbolic significance. It became "foolishness to Greeks and a stumbling-block to Jews," but to Christians, the "wisdom and power of God" (cf. 1 Corinthians 1:23-24). It became a symbol of the self-denial and acceptance of suffering that characterize the Christian vocation. It became the sign of that sharing in Christ's sacrifice that must precede sharing in His Resurrection.

Jesus asks us to share His suffering. He asks us to embrace His cross. He warns that unless we are willing to carry the crosses that He sends us and to follow Him, we will have no part in the eternal life that He has prepared for us. For only through self-denial and self-giving do we truly preserve our lives. Only through following Jesus on the Via Crucis, and so becoming an "everlasting offering" to the Father in Christ's name, can we enter the heaven of faithful servants.

What does our cross consist of? There are as many crosses as there are individuals — plenty to go around. Some examples:

The alcoholic's cross consists partly of not drinking; what a powerful offering to God this can become, when a person whose addiction is in remission abstains from alcohol and so becomes an offering to God and a witness to others.

A person in an unhappy marriage may be called upon to persist in that marriage, to bear that unhappiness, to fulfill the marriage vows and to protect the children — for children are always harmed by divorce. Christ promises no easy way out.

If you lose your job, this is part of the cross that God is asking you to bear (just as He also asks you to carry the burden of seeking new work with faith and trust).

Very often illness forms part of the cross. A chronic or even terminal illness borne with faith and offered to God in atonement for one's own sins and the sins of others can be our way of joining Jesus in His suffering. Suffering then becomes sanctified. Likewise, those whose loved ones die carry a heavy load. They should look forward to their day of reward, however, for Jesus teaches, "Blessed are they who mourn, for they shall be comforted" (Matthew 5:4).

What of the good Catholic woman whose son is found guilty of serious crime? His imprisonment is a heavy part of the mother's cross. Though Jesus was innocent, He carried the instrument of his own execution; and His Mother, who met Him on the way, carried that load vicariously. Many saintly women bear the burden of seeing their children suffer. Our children may not be innocent, but we can still resemble Mary in accepting their punishment.

Are you a parent whose children have left the Church? If so, Jesus asks you to keep them before the altar in your prayers, to be ever more faithful yourself, and to trust in God's goodness. Many parents bear this cross.

Listing the types of cross would be endless. Part of each person's vocation is to carry the cross that Jesus sends, so the number of crosses equals the number of people. Crosses are never simple in their composition, however, just as they are never simple to lift and carry. The meaning of "my cross" is not a single thing, but a composite one. "My cross" is *all* the difficulties that God asks me to accept, especially those that result from my effort to follow Christ. Often these involve ridicule and ostracism; unbelievers scoff at believers more and more in this secularizing society. Less often, but still far too frequently, the cross is the pain of real persecution — oppressive laws, punishment, even death. The century that has just ended saw more Christian martyrs than all previous centuries combined. But unless we are willing to lose our lives for Christ, we will have no eternal life in Him.

Self-denial and acceptance of adversity in the name of Him who denied Himself completely and freely accepted His suffering and death: these are the essential elements of the cross. Self-denial involves yielding our will, first to the Father, and then to our neighbor. "I did it my way" is the song of a fool. Acceptance does not at all mean a frowning, whining attitude. On the contrary, true acceptance of adversity involves cheerfulness, even joy. When we bear the burdens that God sends us with gratitude and praise, we follow the steps of the Master. Accordingly, we will share in His eternal gladness.

Mary's role. Mary met Jesus as He walked toward His death. At that moment, all of the meaning of sharing the cross became a reality for her. What pain she felt. Perhaps even great confusion. Was not her Son treading the path of defeat? What had become of the great promise of His life? And yet she held onto the knowledge that God would somehow make all things new — that her Firstborn would somehow come to victory. With the Blessed Virgin, whom Jesus met on that sorrowful journey to Golgotha, let us renounce ourselves and reflect on the great sacrifice that has brought salvation to us. And like her let us look forward with faith and hope to renewed life beyond the cross.

Intention. We pray that we may always lift and carry the crosses that Jesus sends us, so that we may come to the life He promises. We pray that our sins and enmities, nailed to His cross, may no longer drag us down into gloom or despair. Lord Jesus, we pray that we may take up our crosses and follow you. Amen.

5. The Crucifixion

The biblical scene. According to St. Luke, when the soldiers came with Jesus to Golgotha, "There they crucified him, and the criminals, one on the right and one on the left" (Luke 23:33). St. Mark mentions the offer of a weak anesthetic: "They offered him wine mingled with myrrh; but he did not take it" (Mark 15:23). St. Matthew adds another element: "They offered him wine to drink, mingled with gall; but when he tasted it, he would not drink it. And when they had crucified him, they divided his garments among them by casting lots; they sat down and kept watch over him there" (Matthew 27:34-36).

The Crucifixion is the fulfillment of Jesus' mission. It is the culmination of His self-giving, for, humanly speaking, He has no more to give. He has given His teaching and all His time to the establishment of the Kingdom. He has spoken with divinely penetrating wisdom to the chosen race, most of whom have rejected Him (just as, in fact, most people in almost all societies reject Him when the "cost of discipleship" becomes high). He — the Great Physician — has healed the sick. He who is the Bread of Angels has fed the hungry. As the one true Master, He has taught the real, underlying meaning of the ancient Scriptures. The Man who is "the way, the truth, and the life" (John 14:6) has raised the dead. And now He faces death Himself. Death not in the course of nature but judicially and wrongfully imposed. A death that makes no compromises with suffering or human dignity, but that is designed to exact the most pain and the greatest humiliation. Death on crossed boards on a hilltop — a bloody spectacle of pitilessly imposed misery held up like Moses' serpent before all the people (cf. John 3:14-15, Numbers 21:9).

And with the same miraculous healing promise as that

snake. For when Jesus arises triumphantly on the third day, He becomes the proof of our future resurrection — a divine promise beyond human capacity. But for now, on the cross the vital energy that has led Him to pursue His saving ministry with consuming zeal for God's Kingdom is spent. In a subordinate clause St. Matthew passes over the actual event of the Crucifixion: "and when they had crucified him...." It is as if the killing of the Savior were subordinate to the division of His clothes. Those soldiers had a frugal streak, for they didn't want to waste garments that their owner wouldn't need; and cloth, after all, was expensive. So the focus is on rolling dice for Jesus' robe, while He looms crucified and subordinate in the background. His disciples, who had all fled, must have seen from afar the ignominy that they had avoided. And for the moment, they must have felt an uncomfortable, compromised relief.

On the cross the Lord's body is emptied of His blood. He suffocates gradually, as He becomes tireder and tireder, more and more unable to push Himself up in order to breathe. He speaks a few words — about forgiveness, about thirst, about the repentant thief's reward. He arranges for the care of His Mother, and simultaneously for the marvelous maternal care of His Church for all time. Then, mustering His remaining ounce of energy, He cries out and yields up His spirit. He dies, as does every human being when the soul leaves the body, and the bodily functions, no longer directed, cease. The mortal remains return to earth. So completely did God the Son accept the human condition.

What is our part in the Crucifixion? How do we explain the inescapable fact that it was carried out as a result of our sins and for our benefit? Throughout the ages, the Church has meditated on these questions. For instance: In the prayer *Anima Christi*, used by St. Ignatius in the *Spiritual Exercises*, we find this line, addressed to the crucified Jesus: "In your wounds hide me." How does the Crucifixion *benefit* us? By giving us passage to eternal life. In an almost shocking figure of speech, the *Anima Christi* affirms that it is in the suffering — *in the wounds* — of Christ that we find our safety. The entire Passion, seen as the chief event of God's self-giving grace, is here represented by the wounds of Christ. Through those wounds we are cleansed, as by His stripes we are healed. Through those wounds our sins are forgiven. Because of the Passion of Christ we have the hope of rising to new life and, purged of our mortal stains, being able to stand at God's right hand in the great Judgment. Only in and through the blood that Christ shed can we be reconciled with the Father, whom we have rejected by our disobedience. Only hidden in His wounds can we be carried to heaven.

Well did St. Thomas Aquinas say that contemplation of the crucifix is more valuable than all philosophy. For Christ crucified is the wisdom and power of God.

Mary's role. At the foot of the cross stood the sorrowful Virgin Mary, her heart pierced by the sword of grief. St. Simeon's dark prophecy at the Presentation was thus fulfilled. The seed of spiritual agony planted long before in the mind of the young Mother has come to full flower. Mary stands bereaved, aghast at what has been done to her Son. With her is St. John. Her Firstborn, her only child, wanting in the absence of siblings to take care of His beloved Mother, speaks from the cross, giving her a new son and giving John a new mother: "Woman, behold your son.... Behold your mother" (John 19:26-27). John thus becomes Mary's adopted son, and with him the whole Church and the whole human race become children of Mary.

From the cross, Jesus thus presents to all of His human brothers and sisters a very great gift — next to His own sacrifice, the greatest gift possible. He gives us His own Mother, who prays for us with maternal concern. As Mary presented Jesus to His Father, she presents us to God by her motherly intercession. As she received Jesus in her arms when He was taken down from the cross — God as it were returning the sacrificial Lamb to the woman who gave Him up — so may we repose in the arms of the Blessed Virgin — "now and at the hour of our death."

Intention. "In your wounds hide me," Lord Jesus, for in them I am protected. Like the psalmist who praised life in the shadow of the Almighty (Psalm 91), I find in the wounds of Christ a sure defense against all the enemies of my soul — my own rebellious nature, persecution by Godless people, and the ornate, enticing lures of Satan. We pray that we and all people to whom our lives and prayers pertain may come to eternal life in the wounds of Christ. Amen.

The Glorious Mysteries

1. Christ's Resurrection from the Dead

The biblical scene. Against the overwhelming sorrow and pain, against the noonday shadow of the Crucifixion, appears the brightest light ever to shine in human darkness: Jesus' Resurrection from the dead. St. Mark's account:

> When the sabbath was past, Mary Magdalene, and Mary the mother of James, and Salome, bought spices so that they might go and anoint him. And very early on the first day of the week they went to the tomb when the sun had risen. And they were saying to one another, "Who will roll away the stone for us from the door of the tomb?" And looking up, they saw that the stone was rolled back; for it was very large. And entering the tomb, they saw a young man sitting on the right side, dressed in a white robe; and they were amazed. And he said to them, "Do not be amazed; you seek Jesus of Nazareth, who was crucified. He has risen, he is not here; see the place where they laid him. But go, tell his disciples and Peter that he is going before you to Galilee; there you will see him, as he told you." And they went out and fled from the tomb; for trembling and astonishment had come upon them; and they said nothing to anyone, for they were afraid (Mark 16:1-8).

Here's a sort of syllogism: Human salvation hangs on Christ's divinity. Christ's divinity hangs on His Resurrection. Therefore human salvation hangs on Christ's Resurrection.

What if Jesus had not risen from the dead? What if — after all the evident miracles, after all the profound teaching, after all the plotting against Him and the culminating injustice of His trial and execution — He had simply remained dead? It would mean that the miracles only seemed like miracles, for they didn't come from God. It would mean that the virgin birth was just a pious hoax. It would mean that Christ's followers had been hoodwinked into believing nonsense about Him. Above all, it would mean that our hope for our own resurrection is nothing but a cruel illusion.

Why? Because Jesus' Resurrection demonstrates His divinity as nothing else could. Was He truly the Son of God and the Son of a Virgin? The Resurrection says so. Did He have the right and the power to forgive sins? The Resurrection says so. Were His miracles true interventions of divine power into the laws of nature? The Resurrection so attests. On Jesus' Resurrection depend all His claims of divinity, affirmed by Jesus and His disciples alike. If He didn't rise, He was not God. If He didn't rise, His followers are all just fools and the Church is a monstrous sham. "If Christ has not been raised," says St. Paul, "then our preaching is in vain and your faith is in vain" (1 Corinthians 15:14).

But what does His Resurrection mean? After the Transfiguration, Jesus' disciples debated among themselves just what "rise from the dead" meant (cf. Mark 9:10). Their confusion was fully justified, for they had no empirical precedent to observe and no very clear traditional teaching. The idea of rising from the dead — and the idea of human immortality — had been expressed in Scripture with increasing insistence. Daniel had written about it (cf. Daniel 12:3). Some of the psalms had expressed it — for example, Psalm 17. The books of Wisdom and Maccabees had definitely taught it. Still, who had ever seen it? There was no example of an actual resurrection, though Jesus Himself had resuscitated Lazarus.

People still feel confusion about the Resurrection. And rightly so, for it is a great mystery. Nevertheless, the Church has infallibly taught some truths on the subject. Mysteries yes, but truths nonetheless. Above all, we must understand that Jesus rose *in His true body* from the dead. His Resurrection was no mere survival of His consciousness. It was no merely spiritual affair. St. Augustine teaches that a complete human being is both body and soul, and that body and soul will be reunited in the general resurrection at the end of time. For this splendid event, Jesus is our only clear precedent. (The Blessed Virgin's passing from earthly life has often been called a dormition, or going to sleep, rather than a death. Pope John Paul II, however, made it clear on more than one occasion that Mary was not spared, any more than her divine Son was, from the common fate of us all, viz. death. That said, the Church has always taught that her body did not undergo corruption. The Old Testament prophet Elijah is said to have been taken up to heaven in a whirlwind [2 Kings 2:11]. Whatever happened to them, their entrance into heaven depended on Christ's Resurrection.) Jesus' body and His soul were reunited on the first Easter morning. Our bodies and our souls will be similarly reunited before the great, final Judgment. If God had meant to teach a merely spiritual resurrection, He would not have told us of an empty tomb. And He would not have inspired the Church's belief in a *resurrection* at all, for the survival of consciousness after death is not a resurrection. No. He taught, as the Creed expresses, the "resurrection of the body." And Christ's was the first body to rise. He is the "firstfruits of those who have fallen asleep" (1 Corinthians 15:20).

That is what "resurrection" means. We may not fully understand it. But we accept it as an article of faith because the Holy

Spirit teaches it, first about Jesus and then about us all. Christ's true Resurrection from the dead affirms the divinity of His origin and mission, and points forward to our own resurrection as complete human beings renewed in God's image.

The Resurrection of Christ brings the hope of eternal life to the whole human race. Even those who have never heard of Jesus, if they seek to know and serve God, can come to salvation through Him who harrowed hell and conquered death. Sin and death reigned supreme from the time of Adam to the birth of Christ. But Jesus, in His Resurrection, brought death to death itself, and hope to the whole world. As one poet says, "Death, thou shalt die."

In the fact of Jesus' Resurrection all of the obscure prophecies of the Old Testament about the resurrection of the dead are made clear. The psalmist had written, "I in justice shall behold your face; on waking, I shall be content in your presence" (Psalm 17:15, New American Bible). And, "Man, for all his splendor, if he have not prudence, resembles the beasts that perish" (Psalm 49:21). The prophet Daniel foretold a time when "many" shall rise from the dead (Daniel 12:3). The understanding of human immortality became clearer throughout Old Testament times, and was brought to completion in Christ's victory over death.

And then? Daniel also predicts a Judgment Day, after which some souls will shine like stars and others will be "an everlasting horror and disgrace" (Daniel 12:2, New American Bible). We look to Jesus, who has passed through the change that we call death. He is forever alive. He has shown us the glory that awaits His faithful servants. He has also promised a renewed and everlasting suffering called death to those who die in rebellion against God. How do we avoid that worst catastrophe of all? We look with great hope to the Conqueror of death, and seek to serve Him with true fear of God. We strive to obey all His commands, to enter ever more deeply into His word, so that His truth can set us free from that ancient enemy, mortality, the spawn of satanic temptation and human rebellion against God. Surely, as St. Peter writes, those who so strive in Christ for their own salvation will not be disappointed (cf. 2 Peter 1:10-11).

Mary's role. For our Blessed Mother, the Resurrection of Jesus was the confirmation of hope. She had doubtlessly wondered just how God was going to fulfill the promises made to her about the infant Christ — promises whose fulfillment was obscured by the evident defeat of Jesus' mission on earth. The Resurrection brought the embers of hope back to life. Also, for Mary as for the rest of the human race, Jesus' Resurrection was evidence of future events. For us, the general resurrection. For her — free as she was of the sin that weighs us down — the Assumption. Mary, the holy one of Christ, was not to see the corruption that ordinary people will see. Nevertheless, she had to pass from a creaturely condition to a recreated one in Him. And that change was presaged by His own Resurrection. Let us pray to the Blessed Virgin to be with us in our death, so that we may be with her in our resurrection.

Intention. Well did the medieval dramatists see the glory of this Easter mystery. "Whom do you seek in the tomb?" asks an angel in an ancient Church play. "Jesus," answer the women. *"Non est hic. Surrexit,"* declares the angel: "He is not here. He is risen." And upon hearing this fact, the Church has sung "Alleluia, alleluia" for two thousand years. May the souls of the faithful departed, by the mercy of God, rest in peace as they await the resurrection of their bodies. May the Lord grant that, aided by the prayers of the Mother of God, we may all come to share the glory of His Resurrection. Amen.

2. The Ascension

St. Mark and St. Luke record the Ascension of Christ to heaven. In both versions, the Lord is in the company of the remaining eleven apostles. St. Mark writes, "The Lord Jesus, after he had spoken to them, was taken up into heaven, and sat down at the right hand of God" (Mark 16:19). St Luke is more explicit about the setting: "Then he led them out as far as Bethany, and lifting up his hand he blessed them. While he blessed them, he parted from them, and was carried up into heaven" (Luke 24:50-51).

The disciples so much loved their life with Jesus, and had such great affection for Him personally, that they could hardly bear for Him to leave them. And yet He told them that great benefits would come to them if He ascended to His Father. He would "prepare a place" for them, and by implication for all of us (John 14:3). He would send the Holy Spirit to guide them in their continued discipleship (John 15:26). And in the Church's teaching, He would become the sinner's chief advocate before the Father: "If we sin," St. John writes, "We have an Advocate with the Father, Jesus Christ the righteous" (1 John 2:1). So very much was at stake in the Ascension. And the benefits of it come indeed to all Christ's faithful.

In an anthropomorphic picture, Jesus ascended to heaven and "sat down at the right hand of God." We don't object to anthropomorphism — talking about God in human terms — because, being human, we have no other language. Of course Jesus doesn't actually sit on a throne. (Or does He? After all, He is both body and soul, the complete spiritualized human being who lives forever. Is He in a *place*? Does He sit or stand? So much that the Church teaches about eternity is mysterious.) The important point for us to remember is that Jesus' advocacy and His agency are eternal. They had no beginning, and they will have no end. He is forever our Advocate before the Father. Though we know the Ascension as a historical event, its meaning is not so limited. Jesus is and has always been the Father's chief Agent — His "right-hand man." Just as He was "begotten before all ages," as the Creed states, He has sat at the Father's right hand forever. That is, He has been the Father's chief agent forever. That means that the Anointed Son, with the Father and the Holy Spirit, created the heavens and the earth. Christ led the Israelites and inspired their Scriptures. He entered into the Virgin's womb and "became man." And later — in a historical event that was emblematic of His eternal role — He returned to the Father to plead for His friends on earth.

The parting of the risen Lord from His disciples may have come to them as a surprise. Certainly they objected to it. Just as they had not known what to expect from Him before the Crucifixion, they were confused about what was to come after the Resurrection. Wouldn't Jesus bring about the Kingdom *on earth* now? After all, He was transformed into a spiritual body, no longer subject to death; He would have seemed the perfect leader to transform the world. But God's plan was different. His presence on the earth was to be mediated by the Church, led by the Holy Spirit. Instead of ruling in person, Jesus delegated the governance of His Body to the apostles and their successors. He promised to send the Spirit to guide them. And He ascended to the right hand of the Father, where He is the "one mediator between God and men" (1 Timothy 2:5).

The book of Hebrews describes Christ's entrance into heaven as a permanent entry into the Holy of Holies, the place of the presence of the Father foreshadowed by the Holy of Holies in the ancient Temple. Jesus, the true High Priest — who never has to offer sacrifice again, since He has sacrificed Himself once and for all time — now dwells eternally in the presence of the

Lord God of Hosts. There He is the chief agent — sitting at the "right hand," the hand of action — of the Creator. In other words, He resumes the position He held before all ages — that of the eternally begotten Son, the wise and strong Word, through whom, as St. John says, "all things were made" (John 1:3).

Mary's role. Around the throne of the Lamb are gathered the holy men and women of all times, with Mary as their leader and model. These lesser beings join their much smaller voices to that of the Son. By His grace, their voices are heard, and are powerful in bringing aid to the Church on earth, and to the individuals for whom they pray. Thus in the Communion of Saints these saved souls, who have "kept the faith" and "fought the good fight" (2 Timothy 4:7), share spiritual goods with their earthly brothers and sisters. Some gave their lives for Christ. Some wrote wise books. Some donated their lives to the poor. All shared in the sacrament of the altar, our own spiritual food; all ate the Bread of Angels. All exhibited heroic virtue. Now they raise a great chorus of praise and petition for their struggling friends on earth. In so doing, they lift *us* up to the throne of the Lamb.

Intention. Jesus has represented all the saints before the Father, just as He represents us. He has transformed their sacrifices, made in His name, into worthy offerings to God. In Christ's blood these, His faithful disciples, have won the great victory over sin and death. Now — in solidarity with the Church on earth — the saints sing songs of praise to God and of pleading for us. They keep our interests in the eternal chorus that sounds forever in the presence of our heavenly Advocate. Heaven thus touches earth. This sharing of spiritual goods with us is the essence of the Communion of Saints. Let us offer this decade of the Rosary in gratitude for this communion. Let us give thanks for the Communion of the Saints, who, with Mary at their head, praise Jesus forever and intercede for us until, by His grace, we join them. Amen.

3. The Descent of the Holy Spirit

On the Jewish feast of Pentecost — the first one after Jesus' Resurrection and Ascension — the Holy Spirit was sent from the Father and the Son to inspire the beginning of the Church. The story is told in the book of Acts:

> When the day of Pentecost had come, they were all together in one place. And suddenly a sound came from heaven like the rush of a mighty wind, and it filled all the house where they were sitting. And there appeared to them tongues as of fire, distributed and resting on each one of them. And they were all filled with the Holy Spirit and began to speak in other tongues, as the Spirit gave them utterance (Acts 2:1-4).

The Holy Spirit has never left off His work. As He is eternally the bond between the Father and the Son, He is still the bond between the Church and the Son, and between the Church and the Father. He permeates the Body of Christ, the Church, and moves that body with responsive love for her Savior. He guides her in her thinking, and inspires her to live in self-sacrificing service to mankind — even when individual members of the Church fail to live up to this divine guidance. The Holy Spirit binds God and man together.

Who is this "they" who were "all together in one place" when the Spirit descended? It is at least the apostles and the Virgin Mary. But it is the apostles who receive the new inspiration. They need it. Jesus has left them. When He departed, He gave them a commission: "Go and teach all nations" (Matthew 28:18). But the apostles that we saw recently, at the Crucifixion, could hardly be relied upon to go anywhere besides away, or do anything besides tremble. They were scattered in confusion. They needed transformation. They needed to be reborn in the Spirit of God; to be released from their fears and inhibitions. They also needed new knowledge and understanding.

The whirl of recent events had been very difficult for the apostles to assimilate. Jesus' closest followers and friends failed to understand what He was doing when He journeyed to Jerusalem, toward His death. And they failed to understand the meaning of the phrase "rise from the dead" (Mark 9:10). Now that the stupendous miracle of Christ's Resurrection has taken place, the apostles are in clear need of new understanding, of true comprehension of what they have witnessed. So the Holy Spirit gives them not only courage, but understanding; not only bravery, but also the content of their divine message. (See the account of the Finding in the Temple, above, for the gifts of the Holy Spirit.)

Such was the effect of the Holy Spirit on Peter, Andrew, James, John, and the rest. The change is palpable. St. Peter, for instance — no longer the timorous mouse who fled from Golgotha in fear that a servant girl would get him in trouble — stands up as the leader of the disciples. Though he has hardly realized it before, he has been primed for the role. Perhaps mainly because of his age, he has been the apostles' spokesman from the beginning. Jesus has given him the keys of the Kingdom — a gift that St. Peter cannot understand or use until Pentecost. But now, by the working of the Holy Spirit, he is able to tell the multitude the meaning of the startling events they have witnessed. His fear is gone. His foggy understanding has cleared.

The beginning of the Church on Pentecost involved confronting a horde of enemies. How does St. Peter do this? With shining courage (one of the gifts of the Holy Spirit), he preaches that Jesus is the fulfillment of the ancient prophecy to David. (This is also a principal message of the Joyful Mysteries.) He makes it clear that his colleagues are not drunk, as some have charged, but that the miracles they are beginning to work (the first of which was speaking in tongues) are possible only because Jesus Christ is *still with them*. These signs are proof of the divine presence. And when St. Peter identifies that presence as the very Jesus whom the crowd has caused to be crucified, his auditors are "cut to the heart" and ask what they can do to be saved. Talk about Spirit-filled preaching! "About three thousand" were baptized on Pentecost, including many of those who had conspired in the Lord's death. Without the Holy Spirit, who guides the preacher and the listeners, such an overwhelming result could not have occurred. Here is the Holy Spirit conducting the beginning of the Church. This event is the answer to Christ's prayer from the cross that His tormentors might be forgiven. They are not only reconciled with God, but are made members of the Body of Christ.

The great crowd was moved and, by God's grace, saved. But what are the effects of the Holy Spirit on individuals now, including us? We pray often to the Holy Spirit: "Come... fill the hearts of your faithful and kindle in them the fire of your love." We pray that the Holy Spirit will affect us individually. The petition is, first, for an internal grace. We ask for hearts that will be moved by God's Spirit, so that our obedience to the Lord will be sanctified by grace not only from above, but from within. We are the temples of the Holy Spirit (1 Corinthians 6:19), and when we let Him guide our lives, we show God's love in action — not just in external conformity to commands, but in the goodness that His grace causes to flow from within us.

It is important to remember that the Holy Spirit is not an emotion, and His action in our lives is not primarily an emotional one. Many enthusiastic Christians think of the Holy Spirit as a strong, uplifted feeling within themselves. This *may* be His effect on us *sometimes*, but it certainly isn't necessarily so. Although we want to feel inspired, and though God often gives us this comfort, such a feeling is not an essential part of life in the Spirit. In fact, the obedience to which the Spirit leads can often be painful. It can seem like drudgery, or like a burden, or like a humdrum, repetitive activity. In can, in fact, seem like the cross. So what else should we expect? We must also remember that not every burst of high self-esteem is an indication of the presence of the Spirit. Often we are misled, especially by our own emotions and the seeming goodness of a wrong course of action. At such times we must, as the saints teach, discern among spirits. And then we must follow the Holy Spirit, even if doing so is not so pleasant. Sure, we will often receive the consolations that God gives His true followers. But by no means always. If we take the dry periods with the lush ones, the ultimate result will be greater joy than we can imagine. But for the moment, the Spirit often asks us to postpone that joy in order to follow the will of God rather than our own desires.

How to discern among spirits? For Catholics, the process is often relatively simple. If some spirit prompts you to do something or teach something or believe something that is in conflict with the true teachings of the Church, that spirit is *not* holy. No matter how right a temptation to sin *feels*, it is wrong and comes from the devil. No matter how inconvenient a moral teaching of the Church sometimes is (as supposedly in the case of contraception), that teaching comes from the Holy Spirit and is to be obeyed. No matter how culturally foreign or strange a Church doctrine may seem (as in the perpetual virginity of our Blessed Mother), all solemn teachings of the Church come from the Holy Spirit and are to be humbly received. This is the great guarantee of Christ to His Church: that He will be with her for all time, and will teach and guide her by His Holy Spirit. Let us obey Him.

Mary's role. Pentecost is the climactic event in the transformation of the apostles. Most of them had run away from the

Crucifixion, fearful and doubtful. But Christ's Resurrection removed their doubts, and now the Holy Spirit eradicates their fears. As a result, they are able to speak boldly in the name of Christ, without worrying about the consequences. Nearly all were eventually martyred, but not before they had ordained bishops to succeed them. In steps: The Church began to take its permanent shape when Jesus gave the keys to St. Peter. The first body of Christians was baptized in Jerusalem on Pentecost, and then dispersed throughout the Mediterranean world to carry the teaching of the apostles. The permanent structure of the Church, with Peter at the head as the Vicar of Christ, and with the apostles and their successor bishops as authoritative teachers of Sacred Tradition, quickly took shape. What a miracle was wrought on Pentecost! Only the power of God could have brought it about, and only He could have maintained the resulting institution, the Bride of Christ, for the succeeding 2,000 years.

The Blessed Virgin was there, of course. But did the Holy Spirit descend upon her as on the apostles? We don't know for sure, but I think not. Surely she had already received a full measure of the Holy Spirit, for the Spirit was her Spouse, who begot her Firstborn. Mary was already the Queen of the apostles, the adoptive Mother of Jesus' companions. Now she takes her place as the Mother of the nascent Church, already sanctified, already holy — already taught daily for thirty-three years by the Son of God.

Intention. Let us ask Mary to help us always follow the guidance of the Holy Spirit, who expresses Himself chiefly through the teachings of the Catholic Church. By her intercession, she will obtain for us the grace to live holy lives and to join her in heaven someday. Amen.

4. The Assumption of the Blessed Virgin

The doctrinal and biblical record. On November 1, 1950, Pope Pius XII defined the dogma of the Assumption:

> by the authority of our Lord Jesus Christ, of the Blessed Apostles Peter and Paul, and by our own authority, we pronounce, declare, and define it to be a divinely revealed dogma: that the Immaculate Mother of God, the ever Virgin Mary, having completed the course of her earthly life, was assumed body and soul into heavenly glory (*Munificentissimus Deus*, 44).

More than some of the other mysteries, the Assumption may seem strange to us. I remember a good Catholic friend once saying that he had a warm feeling about all the mysteries of the Rosary except for the Assumption. What is it about, he asked, and what does it have to do with me? My answer — about which I had never thought; it must have come somehow from the Holy Spirit — was that the Assumption was Jesus' way of honoring His Mother, and that this mystery asks us to honor her too. My friend seemed satisfied.

Of course, there's much more to the Assumption than that. In the document defining this dogma, the Holy Father strongly taught that the Assumption is part of Sacred Tradition. Contrary to what some people thought at the time, this doctrine wasn't a recent invention of a fantasizing Church. Affirming the Blessed Virgin's translation into heaven was a confirmation of what Catholics had believed since the Church was new.

All teaching about Mary comes, one way or another, from God's revelation regarding His Son. For centuries the Church reasoned that God would not — could not — have chosen an impure vessel to bear the Savior into the world. So Pope Pius IX, reaffirming Sacred Tradition, defined the dogma of the Immaculate Conception. That definition was necessary. Logic compelled it, growing as the doctrine did from the Church's belief in the divinity and Resurrection of Christ. But then, 100 years later, logic again compelled a definition of Marian dogma. If Mary was born free of original sin (as the dogma of the Immaculate Conception teaches), then how could she suffer the ordinary death and corruption that resulted from sin? No sin, no corruption. Right from the earliest times that Christians began to think about who Mary is — with relation to Jesus Christ — they had believed that Mary could not have decomposed in the grave. They believed, rather, that her death was merely an instantaneous going to sleep, a "dormition," and that, following her death, she was immediately changed into a spiritual body and taken to heaven, where she is highly honored. Christ's Resurrection proves it, and Mary's Assumption confirms it: We will all be changed into *spiritual bodies*, either at the general resurrection or at the last trumpet announcing Christ's Second Coming. Reunited then with the eternal consciousness that we call the soul, we will be complete human beings, ready for Judgment. We all have to wait for this, except for Mary (and the prophet Elijah). For the sinless Mother of God was assumed into heaven not too long after Jesus ascended to His Father. He had gone ahead and "prepared a place" for her, just as He is preparing a place for us.

In *Munificentissimus Deus*, Pope Pius XII remarked that "the two dogmas [the Immaculate Conception and the Assumption] are intimately connected in close bond." They are based on "two very singular privileges bestowed upon the Virgin Mother of God... as the beginning and as the end of her earthly journey; for the greatest possible glorification of her virgin body is the complement, at once appropriate and marvelous, of the absolute innocence of her soul, which was free from all stain." This is an inspired summary of the theology of the Assumption.

Also, the Assumption continues the submission that the Son shows to His Mother on earth. Both before and after the Finding in the Temple, He *obeyed* her. Honoring Mary was a part of the life of Jesus, who lived by the commandments every day. The final mysteries of the Rosary are a further expression of Jesus' filial desire to honor His Virgin Mother. He not only obeyed her as a child, he also began His public ministry of miracles at her bidding at the wedding at Cana; now at the end of her earthly life, He further exalts her. Obviously, Mary's maternal influence on her Son is very powerful. We should follow the wedding guests at Cana and go "to Jesus through Mary."

Mary's role. The Blessed Virgin has a "starring role" in the Assumption. Whereas the previous Glorious Mysteries focus on Jesus, in the Assumption Mary is in the foreground. We still reflect on what Jesus did for her. We are still very much aware that the Assumption resulted from the divinity of Christ. Consequently, we still regard Jesus as Lord and God, and Mary as a creature.

But these facts merely underline one of the inner meanings of the Assumption. That is: If we want to be more like Christ, we will join Him in honoring Mary, and the steadfast purity and faith that she embodied. We will see how glory finally comes to those who give themselves completely to Him. And, though we know that we are by no means immaculate, we look forward to our life with the Blessed Virgin in that glorious realm.

Intention. Let us pray that we may follow Mary in bearing witness to Christ, no matter what the cost; that we may join Him in honoring His Mother as He did (to the best of our ability); and that we may always rely upon her maternal help. Let us pray that we may faithfully fulfill the roles to which we are called as Mary's children: that we may become and remain the kind of children she wants for her own. Amen.

5. The Coronation of the Virgin in Heaven

The doctrinal and biblical record. The Church links the Coronation closely with the Assumption. According to Vatican II, the "Immaculate Virgin, preserved free from all stain of original sin, was taken up body and soul into heavenly glory when her life was over, and exalted by the Lord as Queen over all things, that she might be the more fully conformed to her Son, the Lord of lords and conqueror of sin and death" (*Dogmatic Constitution on the Church*, 59). The taking up and the exaltation are two parts of the same process, that of rewarding Mary for her faithfulness and making her the model for all Christians. We look to her as the "model of virtues" who "prompts the faithful to come to her Son" (Ibid., 65).

As the Mother of the Lamb of God, Mary is the agent who brings the New Covenant to fruition. The reward that she gets for this saving work, embodied in the Assumption and Coronation, is symbolically represented in Scripture. In the book of Revelation appears a celestial woman who wears a crown of twelve stars, corresponding to the twelve tribes of Israel and the twelve apostles. In the reading of the Church, the celestial woman is clearly Mary, though she is also the Church. St. John describes her in dramatic and cosmic terms:

> A great portent appeared in heaven, a woman clothed with the sun, with the moon under her feet, and on her head a crown of twelve stars; she was with child and she cried out in her pangs of birth, in anguish for delivery (Revelation 12:1-2).

In the great battle that ensued, St. Michael the Archangel

defeated the red dragon, "that ancient serpent, who is called the Devil and Satan, the deceiver of the whole world" (Revelation 12:9), and cast him down to earth. After the heavenly battle, the enemy turned upon "the woman who had borne the male child." Unable to destroy her, he "went off to make war on the rest of her offspring, on those who keep the commandments of God and bear testimony to Jesus" (Revelation 12:13, 17). Subsequently, those who conquer the dragon do so "by the blood of the Lamb and by the word of their testimony" (Revelation 12:11); that is, by bearing witness to Christ even if it means their death.

We think of Mary as a model. But her queenship makes her more than a model. Like her Son, she embodies a perfection to which we can only aspire. We cannot really imitate it, though we must try. According to Pope Leo XIII, Mary has reached "a height of glory granted to no other creature, whether human or angelic." As "the invincible Queen of Martyrs," she sits in the "heavenly city of God by the side of her Son, crowned for all eternity" (*Magnae Dei Matris* [1892], 25). Nevertheless, the reward that we seek for our devotion to God's will is *analogous* to the honors that Mary receives. We deserve, and will get, less than she received. But it will still be *like* the reward of our Queen: as much of the presence of Christ as we can individually bear, and forever. With it we will be entirely and eternally satisfied. But our righteousness and purity will always be at best a poor shadow of hers. All the more reason for us to strive for perfection.

Pope Pius XII instituted celebration of the Queenship of Mary as a liturgical feast. He points to the antiquity of Mary's title as Queen, just as he notes the ancient tradition of the Assumption. To all the honors accorded her, however, Mary's role as mother is intimately linked. Recent commentators have shown that in the tradition of Israel, the queen mother — the mother of the king, not the wife of the king — is a figure of great power. Mary's motherhood of Jesus, and her universal motherhood of all the children of God, culminate in the honors of her royal reign: "Mary, the Virgin Mother of God, *reigns with a mother's solicitude* over the entire world, just as she is crowned in heavenly blessedness with the glory of a Queen" (*Ad Caeli Reginam* [1954], 1, italics added). Mother and Queen, inseparable, of the heir of David. Many fathers and doctors of the Church had given her queenly dignity and royal titles — "Queen of all creatures, the Queen of the world, and the Ruler of all" — before Pius XII so strongly joined Mary's maternal and royal identities.

Just as Jesus is a very special kind of king, Mary is a very special kind of queen. Christ reigns by being a shepherd, not a boss. The Good Shepherd "lays down His life for the sheep" (John 10:11); He doesn't demean or tyrannize over them. Jesus also reigns by having "all authority" given to Him "in heaven and on earth" (Matthew 28:18), and in the Church's liturgy this authority is manifest in His victory over death as well as in the prophetic expectation that someday "every knee" will bend before Him (Philippians 2:10). Moreover, like the ancient kings, Jesus is both ruler and judge, for at the last day He "will judge the living and the dead" (*Nicene Creed*). In none of these aspects of Christ's kingship do we see the stereotypes of secular kingship. Nor is Mary a stereotypical queen. Her queenship is made of other stuff than earthly royalty. Her reign consists precisely in endorsing and being taken up in Jesus' reign. Her focus is on Him. By the saving grace of God, Mary's reign is the same as Christ's. When we seek the reign of Mary, we seek the reign of Jesus; for He reigns absolutely in her Heart. Just as Mary's earthly life was centered on the will of her Son, her heavenly life is focused on Him. She pleads for us sinners, yes, but she does so in order to help us conform to the divine will, to which she is herself completely obedient. Jesus obeyed His spotless Mother on earth, even to the extent of starting His ministry of miracles at her bidding. But we never forget that His obedience was balanced by her perfect submission to His divine will. Thus the two reigns — of the Sacred Heart of Jesus and the Immaculate Heart of Mary — become one.

Mary's role. When the Blessed Virgin appeared to St. Bernadette at Lourdes, she said "I *am* the Immaculate Conception." She didn't say what seems more logical to us: "I am a *product* of the Immaculate Conception," or "I *came from* the Immaculate Conception." Thus Mary follows in the example of the Son Himself, who says "I am the way, the truth, and the life" (John 14:6). Not "I will show you the way," or "I speak the truth," but "I *am* the way and the truth." There is no division here between actor and role. And so it is with Mary. She is not just a distant image, but the very companion and mediatrix of our salvation: our Queen in heaven and our helper and friend on earth. In Jesus and Mary, image and meaning, actor and role, are identical. That is why knowing Jesus and His Mother is the equivalent of knowing God.

Intention. May Jesus grant that we always honor the Queen of Heaven, who eternally adores her Son and Savior. May we seek her reign in our lives and in all the world and, in so doing, seek the reign of God. May God grant that we always dwell in the grace of His Sacred Heart by loving and serving His Mother, our Queen. Amen.

Reflections Before the Blessed Sacrament

In addition to meditation on the mysteries of the Rosary, we join the Blessed Mother in worship of the Blessed Sacrament, and so ally ourselves with her Immaculate Heart, which is ever turned toward the Sacred Heart of her Son.

Through reflection on the Eucharist — guided by the Holy Spirit to contemplate the Son of God the Father — we encounter the Holy Trinity. Through focusing on Christ's presence, we draw near to Him, listen to Him, and speak to Him. In his late document *Ecclesia de Eucharistia*, Pope John Paul II emphasized that Mary is the Mother of the Eucharist, that when we worship Christ in the Blessed Sacrament, we attend the "school of Mary" and learn devotion at her side. Therefore, let us adore the Blessed Sacrament. Let us kneel with the Blessed Mother and converse with God. Let's go to school.

1. The Presence of Christ

I know that the Holy Eucharist is both the sign and the means of Christ's presence in His Church: the *sign*, since the external appearance of bread and wine *signify* the real substance of the Body and Blood of Christ; the *means*, since the Eucharist is not a symbol, but the reality. Under the sign of bread and wine, the Eucharist brings Jesus Himself — body, blood, soul, and divinity — to His Church. He is before me now. He showed His wounds to St. Thomas in order to say, "It is I, the Lord. I am here. I am with you." So also, to the eyes of faith, He is here on the altar, in flesh, blood, soul, and divinity. Blessed are they who know Christ's presence under these chosen simple signs.

Thus it is with all the sacraments. The Lord Jesus chose common things — water, oil, hands, words, bread, wine — and elevated them to sacramental status. The things themselves are therefore signs, but the reality is the presence of Jesus. Water is the sign of sacramental cleansing from original sin and entrance into the Church. But not only a sign, for in the water and words and motions of Baptism, Jesus is truly present. Jesus, the Christos, the Anointed, is also truly present when the priest anoints the sick with holy oil; as Jesus Himself is the anointed descendant of the anointed king David — Son of David, Son of God, Son of Mary.

In her sacraments the Church brings Jesus to a world starving for Him. Thus the Church, by the grace of God, is the sacrament of salvation that makes the Son of God present to all the world; the vine of Israel that reaches out with grace — with

Jesus — to the whole creation. And the Sacrament of the Altar — the holy Presence before me — is daily food for those who desire to live always in the presence of Christ.

Lord Jesus Christ, I kneel in your presence. The external appearance of bread before me — bread consecrated on your altar, and now bread no more but your resurrected Body — tells me that you are with me and with the whole Church. On how many altars throughout the world are you now visible, present and adored? Before your presence I kneel. With me kneel Mary and all the saints. For through the ages you have been present to the holy men and women who sought to serve you. Through the ages you have been their food and drink, miraculously multiplied on the altars of your Church.

Saints of heaven, lift me and everyone for whom I pray up to the throne of the Lamb. As I kneel before the Bread of Angels, fill me, Lord Jesus, with your Spirit. Give me peace of mind and courage to do your bidding when I leave this altar, that I may carry your sacramental presence with me wherever I go. Amen.

2. Mary, Mother of the Eucharist

As I kneel, you kneel with me, holy Mother of God. I reflect upon the first days of the Church, when you graced the apostles with your company. Then you too ate the Bread of Angels. You had seen Him die, rise from the dead, and ascend into heaven. Afterward, you received your own Son in Holy Communion. From Him you derived the joy of faith, hope, and love as you awaited your reunion with Jesus in heaven.

The resurrected Body of Christ is before me. Mother Mary, this Body was formed in your womb. The angel Gabriel, the messenger of God, came to you long ago in Nazareth and announced that you had been chosen to carry God in your body. With great generosity toward the human race and great humility toward the Almighty, you answered the angel: "Let it be done to me as you say." Thus you expressed your obedient submission to God's will in the presence of His messenger. Thus you reversed the ancient sin of Eve, who had listened to Satan rather than God.

Jesus was formed by the miraculous working of God. He also came from an ovum produced by your own body. Otherwise, the Lord would not have truly been your Son. *O magnum mysterium!* O great mystery! that God should become incarnate in the body of a chaste virgin, and with her cooperation.

For the nine months of your pregnancy Jesus grew in your womb. Your food was His, your bed was His, your journeys were His. Your lodging in the stable in Bethlehem was His. Truly, Mother, "the Lord is with thee." The Body formed in your womb was crucified on Calvary. That Body rose from the dead and ascended into heaven.

But He also stayed with us in the Eucharist. About His continuing presence with His disciples, the Lord Jesus said: "This is my Body." And you, holy Mother of God, formed that Body in your womb by the mysterious power of the Most High. Truly you are the Mother of the Eucharist, and therefore the Mother of the Church, the Mother of the Body of Christ, the Mother of the human race adopted at the Incarnation and on Calvary. Be with me, Mother. I know that you kneel with me as I worship the great gift of the Eucharist, formed in your body and present before me now. Amen.

3. Reparation to the Sacred Heart of Jesus

Lord Jesus, you are both God and Man. You are perfect in your Divinity and in your Humanity. Yet when you lived on earth as a man, you were not above the struggling and suffering people whom you met. Except for sin, you were like your human brothers. You shared your life with your human sisters.

In your humanity, Lord, you knew the pain of failure, of unrequited love, of ingratitude, of futile hopes. And in your most generous Heart, you were hurt by these rejections. Your Sacred Heart is the home of your most earnest desires for our good. From your Sacred Heart poured out the greatest possible love for lost mankind. And yet by my sins I have often rejected this love, just as the citizens of ancient Judea rejected it.

I come before you now, Lord Jesus, to make reparation for the injuries inflicted on your Sacred Heart, well aware that I have done my part in causing you pain. I remember the grief you felt when your countrymen hardened their hearts against you. When you proposed to do good on the Sabbath by healing a man's shrunken hand, your good intentions met with nothing but scorn. It seems that people preferred deformity to your healing miracles — especially if it was someone else's deformity.

I recall how merchants profaned the Temple. You had sought out the Temple, your "Father's house," at the age of twelve. And then the animal-sellers and moneychangers made that house a "den of thieves."

I recall how your own relatives refused your prophetic message. This painful affront to your Sacred Heart — this "lack of faith" — prevented the healing miracles that you might have worked in Nazareth.

I recall how you addressed the cities of Judea, how you

would have gathered them to yourself in your Kingdom, but were met with indifference or hostility. Your countrymen not only rejected the goodness of your Heart, they resolved to kill you.

I recall how you wept at the death of your friend Lazarus. I recall how you suffered in the Garden of Gethsemane. You foresaw your own painful death and, like any man, wanted to avoid it. You were deserted. You were lonely. You were in physical and mental agony. Nevertheless, you deferred to the Father's will in accepting the sacrifice He demanded.

I recall the great sadness with which you looked upon your Mother as she stood before the cross.

I recall that I too am complicit in your death. When men ask, "Who crucified Christ?" I have to answer, "I did."

And so I offer to your Sacred Heart, Lord Jesus, such small reparation as I can make. I resolve in your presence to avoid sin and to do your will in all things, so as not to offer your Heart any more pain than I have already caused. I resolve to return your love. Amen.

4. Reparation to the Immaculate Heart of Mary

Holy Virgin, when you stood before the cross of your Son, your Immaculate Heart broke with pain and grief. When His Heart was pierced, your own Heart was pierced — as Holy Simeon had foretold long ago in the Temple. Pain to His Heart was pain to yours. Joy to Him was joy to you. Your hearts were and are spiritually joined. As a result of this unity of your Heart with the Heart of Christ, you are "full of grace," for Jesus is the source of all grace.

Your Heart is immaculate — spotlessly innocent of all wrongdoing and wrong willing. That purity also comes from the Sacred Heart of Jesus. In His great love for a fallen world, Jesus came into His own creation as a man, a Shepherd, seeking the lost sheep, the race that had renounced its original blessedness and plunged into the "shadow of death." Part of His plan was to make a woman worthy to bear Him into the world — a woman who, free from the darkness of sin, was created immaculate so that she could be a suitable dwelling for the Incarnate God.

You freely accepted this role, Mother Mary. And in that act of obedience, you accepted the vocation of giving yourself totally to the interests of your Son. Your Heart freely embraced the mission, the desires, the intentions, the love for fallen man, the willingness to accept suffering, the principle of sacrifice, of Jesus Christ. In His Sacred Heart are all your motives. In His Sacred Heart is all your concern. Your Immaculate Heart is illumined with the light of His Sacred Heart, as the moon receives the light of the sun.

Consequently, reparation to one Heart is reparation to the

other. As the Lord bore the pain of rejection — the Shepherd spurned by the sheep — you suffered with Him. As, moved by His Sacred Heart, He gave Himself totally for a lost and ungrateful race, you took upon yourself His love for the sinful children that He gave to you in His birth and on the cross. As our sins crown His Heart with thorns, they pierce your Heart with a sword. And so I, who pierced Him on the cross, come to you, holy Mother, in reparation to your Immaculate Heart.

Lord Jesus, before me body and soul in the Holy Eucharist, I come to you now with grateful love to the Immaculate Heart of your Mother. I kneel, Mother, in reparation to your Heart. For I know that your Immaculate Heart is inextricably bound with the Sacred Heart of your Son. When I have rejected Him I have rejected you. When I have hurt Him by my ingratitude and sin, I have hurt you. When I have treated Him with indifference, I have snubbed you. Hear me, holy Mother of God. In your maternal love accept my repentance and offer my sorrow to Jesus, who gave you to me and me to you in a holy adoption. Mother, as you presented Jesus to the Father in the Temple, present me and those for whom I pray, by your motherly intercession. Immaculate Heart of Mary, pray for us. Amen.

5. The Eucharist, Center of the Christian Life

Lord Jesus, with divine authority you taught that you are the Bread of Life. Infinitely superior to manna, another bread given by the Father, you give your people sustenance for eternal life. You promise that whoever eats the Bread of Life in faith will never die. This fact makes you, the Bread of Life, the center not of fleeting but of eternal life — the Bread that preserves body and soul for everlasting health in your presence; imperishable food for imperishable life.

No wonder the Eucharist is the center of life for your faithful servants. For the Sacrament of the Altar is your chosen means of remaining with your Church in body and soul, divinity and humanity. The Eucharist *forms* the Church, as Pope John Paul taught. So members of the Church lead lives *formed* by your Body, which is before me on the altar. Can a life renounce its own form? Can the Church and her members be truly alive without the Eucharist? What else could be the center of our lives?

You, O Lord, are the Way, the Truth, and the Life. You *are* the Life. Not a sign pointing to life, not a symbol of life, not a mere teacher about life. You are the Life. Inasmuch as I remain in you — inasmuch as I draw my vital nourishment from the Bread of Life — I have life.

All around me, as the old song says, I see "change and decay." But in the Holy Eucharist I find food, not for a perishing life in this world, but for life in the City of God. Sure, I live in the City of Man. But it is not my true home. For I am also, and more importantly, a citizen of the City of God. Ordinary food leaves me subject to change and decay, hunger and death. But the Bread of Life anchors my existence in the life that never ends, eternal life in the presence of God.

When I leave the Holy Sacrifice of the Mass, having been fed with the Bread of Life, I carry with me the spiritual sustenance that will last until my next Communion. I carry you with me. I remember where my life is centered. I recall your infinite generosity. My thoughts reach back to the altar. In faith I hearken back to the words of Institution — "This is my Body" — and remember that I bear your Body in myself. Indeed, that as a member of your Church I *am* your Body. You are my center. Could I ever be separated from what I am?

Holy Sacrament of God, Bread of Heaven, be the center of my life. Bring all for whom I pray to center their lives on you. Forgive my sloth and forgetfulness, by which I neglect my true identity. Forgive my sins, by which I evict you from the center of my life and enthrone my own lusts and pride. Recall me now in these devotions to my true center. Help me to remain with you. Grant that I may abide in your presence even when I leave this place; not only today, but forever and ever. Amen.

6. The Peace of the Risen Christ

Lord Jesus, by the eyes of faith I see you on the altar before me. The pale disc in the monstrance, formerly bread "which the earth has given," has been changed into the Bread of Angels — the food that only Heaven can give. Bread no longer, but your very Body. You are there in the candlelight. I visit you here in reparation to your Sacred Heart and the Immaculate Heart of your holy Mother.

Just what do I see before me with the eyes of faith? After your Resurrection you came, Lord, to the upper room. In your transformed, resurrected body, you appeared to your apostles. You said, "Peace be with you." But the peace that you conferred on your apostles was more than an absence of conflict, for it came from One who had passed through the curtain of death and entered the Holy of Holies. Indeed, this is a peace that I can have, by your grace, even in the midst of great earthly conflict. This peace "passes understanding."

When you appeared in that room, your own human conflict was over. Your bitter Passion — betrayal, Gethsemane, trial, mockery, crucifixion, death, all at the hands of the very beneficiaries of your suffering — was ended. You were victorious. You had risen. What a conflict this must have been, to undergo such torment voluntarily. On the cross you had given the last ounce of your blood. You had been taken down dead. You were buried. And then on the third day you arose to new life. Your apostles cowered in fear in the upper room, waiting for some further revelation that they didn't understand. And you returned to them. They saw you.

But St. Thomas wasn't there. Not that time, at least. And because he wasn't there, he didn't believe that the other apostles had seen you. What he wanted was visual proof of your Resurrection. In doing so, he wanted no more than the other apostles had already received. They had seen you. They had had visual proof. Because St. Thomas wanted the same — and, in so wanting, refused to take the mere word of the others, so outlandish was their claim of your Resurrection — we call him "Doubting Thomas." Thus we slight this great apostle and feel slightly superior to him, since we falsely think we would have been more receptive to the apostles' assertion that the impossible had occurred. That the dead had risen.

When you returned the next week, Thomas was there. You gave him the proof he wanted. He saw the holes in your hands and the gash in your side. Not only saw, but felt. He got not only visual but tactile proof. And when he did so, he exclaimed, "My Lord and my God!" And a great peace descended upon all the apostles, who were soon to go out and, except for St. John, imitate your Passion and die as martyrs.

This is what we believe about the little breadlike disc before me: "My Lord and my God!" Through my eyes of faith, you, Lord Jesus, are identical in body, blood, soul, humanity, and divinity to this consecrated host. Bread no more, but my Lord and my God.

Thomas was greatly favored, as had been the other apostles. They actually saw you risen, in the flesh. They saw you in the transformed body that ascended to heaven a few weeks later. They saw you in the changed state miraculously presaged by your Transfiguration. They saw you in your immortal body, a body such as you will give to each of us at the general resurrection. But they *saw* you. In so doing, they knew you as the risen Lord. Their faith had become knowledge. In this they were richly blessed.

You want to bless us too. You said to Thomas, "You believe because you see me. Blessed are they who have not seen, and yet believe." I pray you, Lord, grant me the eyes of a lively faith.

Reflections Before the Blessed Sacrament

Grant that I may always remain among the blessed who see and know you in the most holy Sacrament of the Altar. And grant me that peace that comes from your victory over death — peace retrieved from the Holy of Holies, and given to your people throughout the ages.

> Soul of Christ, sanctify me.
> Body of Christ, save me.
> My Lord and my God.

7. The Benediction of the Blessed Sacrament

A benediction indeed. Lord Jesus, your continued presence is a great blessing. I know of no greater one. You are present in your Church — in her Scriptures, in her members, and in all her sacraments. Your presence is brought home to me by the holy Sacrament that I now adore. There is great benediction here — the giving of a great blessing — from the Exposition of your Body and the singing of "O Salutaris Hostia" ("O Saving Victim") to the great joy and peace that comes when your priest makes the sign of the cross over us with that same Body.

Before your agony in Gethsemane, before the poet's "torchlight red on sweaty faces" at your betrayal, before the mockery and pain of the crown of thorns and your horrendous scourging, before the unjust sentence of death was given or carried out: before all of this, with the greatest forgiveness and self-abnegation ever shown, you consecrated bread and wine as your Body and Blood for your apostles. The forgiveness that you expressed on the cross preceded the cross, just as the institution of the Eucharist preceded your death. Indeed, forgiveness was the whole purpose of your Incarnation. Though you knew about the suffering that you were to receive at our hands, you still wanted to stay with us in the Mass — to show us the great hope to which you were calling us.

In that upper room, you made clear your ardent will to remain with your as-yet-unborn Church in this most wonderful of sacraments, the Sacrament of the Altar. Such mercy and faithfulness astonishes me. For you had left your glory. You had come out from the halls of heaven to plunge into your own creation, and there to suffer at the hands of your own creatures. Amazing it is that with such steadfast love you promised to remain among us in the sign and reality of the Blessed Sacrament. This is a benediction beyond all human logic or imagination.

The elements of the wonderful ceremony of Benediction invite reflection. Incense for your holiness; the song hailing you as the "saving Victim" who opens "wide the gate of heaven"; your Mother's constant presence with you and with us, recalled in the Rosary, the Litany of Loretto, the image of the Immaculate Heart; the minutes and hours of adoration and reflection before you on the altar; the First Saturday reception of the Sacrament of Penance. And then, as befits a blessing beyond words, the wordless sign of the cross made by your priest over your people. Lord, because such a benediction is beyond all human telling, we can do no more than praise the mystery of your presence with a second song of St. Thomas Aquinas — our song of wonder before "so great a sacrament."

I lack all health until I kneel before you. And so I bend my knees before you, Lord, and await the Spirit and life that you alone can impart to me. Your Body, lifted on the cross, shapes the cross over me. Your Body, Blood, Soul, and Divinity will abide with me even when my flesh declines and my senses fail. Your presence gives me peace and hope, as I contemplate your risen Body and look forward with faith to my own resurrection in you — eternal benediction. Amen.

8. The Blessed Sacrament and the Joyful Mysteries

Your presence on the altar before me, Lord Jesus, came about because of your mysterious entry into the created world. This entry took place through the cooperation of your Mother, Mary. The love that you displayed in your Incarnation is beyond my comprehension. Perhaps you could have saved the human race by some other means — by a discarnate means — though the Scripture says that you "had to suffer" (cf. Matthew 16:25, Luke 24:46, Acts 3:18). I don't know. But I do know that you *chose* to be conceived in the womb of a Virgin — who cooperated with the Holy Spirit and humbly submitted to the will of God. And that your conception as a human being cast you in the human condition, subject to all the "shocks that flesh is heir to" (as Hamlet says).

After her initial fear and confusion, the Annunciation was joy itself to the Blessed Virgin. When she was asked to carry you in her body, she too acknowledged the mystery: "How can this be, since I have no husband?" (Luke 1:34). But this much she did know — that she should continue her life of prayer and submission to her Creator by acquiescing in His will: "Let it be done to me according to your word" (Luke 1:38). And the result, according to St. John, was that "The Word became flesh and dwelt among us, full of grace and truth" (John 1:14).

Nurturing the Incarnate God in one's womb, then raising Him in one's home: these are scenes of joy and wonder that we call the Joyful Mysteries. Jesus, true God and true Man, you were made from Mary's body. Engendered by the Holy Spirit, you grew there in the safety and sanctity of her immaculate womb. With her you visited St. Elizabeth and the unborn St. John. She carried you with her to Bethlehem, City of David, where you, the Son of David, Son of God, and Son of Mary, were born in an obscure cave. Thus can God, as the poet Chaucer says, "send His grace even into a little ox's stall."

I marvel at the reality of your life among us. What a decline from heavenly glory. This truly is the fundamental poverty that you voluntarily embraced — not the poverty of lacking earthly possessions, but that of becoming human and becoming, as a man, subject to the frailties and infirmities of the flesh — even death. You became fundamentally poor like us.

From the moment of your conception you were fully human, for it was at the moment of your conception that "the Word became flesh." Acknowledging your full humanity, Lord, even from your invisible beginnings as a man, I pray for a renewed reverence toward innocent human life in my culture and society. Have mercy on us, Lord Jesus, and protect the innocent from intentional destruction. Deliver us from the twin sins of contraception and abortion. Grant that we may always remember you were incarnated as the minutest form of human life in the body of the Virgin — never a *mere* embryo or fetus, but the Word made flesh.

Mother Mary, as you presented Jesus, your Firstborn, to His Father in the Temple, I beg you to present me and everyone for whom I pray. By your maternal intercession, keep us before the throne of God — in the warm light of the Sacred Heart of Jesus and your own Immaculate Heart. Make the Presentation your gift to us. Present us to our Father.

Lord Jesus, when Mary and Joseph found you in the Temple, you were tending to your "Father's business" (cf. Luke 2:49). There, in the presence of the rabbis of Judea, you exhibited in full the gifts of the Holy Spirit. Grant me those same gifts in all my dealings. Grant me wisdom, understanding, knowledge, counsel, courage, piety, and fear of God. Grant, Lord Jesus, that I and all the world may be guided by your Spirit. Mary, Mother of the Eucharist, pray for us. Amen.

9. The Blessed Sacrament and the Luminous Mysteries

Lord Jesus, your entire sojourn in your own creation showed the human race inextinguishable light. Among us as a man, you brought the light of spiritual intellect in your teaching and the light of hope in your saving deeds. You brought your followers out of the shadow of death and into the light of your Resurrection.

In the Luminous Mysteries, or Mysteries of Light, we rejoice in you as the true bearer of light to the world. These mysteries lodge between the unknown years of your youth and the seeming darkness of your Passion. The Luminous Mysteries are the light of your public ministry, scenes enacted for the direct illumination of the human race. Shine on me, Lord. Word of God, be always a lamp for my feet and a light to my path.

I see how prominent the sacraments are in your ministry of light. In the first mystery, you blessed the waters of baptism by letting St. John baptize you. In your own baptism, as the *Jerusalem Catecheses* state, the water was washed: you imparted to the waters of the River Jordan the fragrance of your divinity. This was light. This was the beginning of the sacrament of Baptism, for after your Resurrection, you commissioned your disciples to baptize "all nations" "in the name of the Father, the Son, and the Holy Spirit."

When you humbly submitted to this baptism, you revealed the pattern of all the sacraments. These acts all employ humble things — water, oil, words, bread and wine, the "laying-on of hands" — as both signs and means of your personal presence. You who are before me here on the altar — you made common water into the water of life, which washes sin away and opens the door to your Church; which immerses the baptismal candidate into your saving death and lifts him up to the light of your Resurrection. I thank you, Lord, for the sacrament of Baptism.

At Cana in Galilee, you prefigured the Eucharist by turning water into wine. Water of baptism, water turned into wine: another way of lifting this common life-element above its own nature. Thus you began your public ministry of miracles, at the invitation of your Virgin Mother. At that wedding you also blessed the sacrament of Matrimony. You lifted this ancient, divinely instituted, but common human bond to the status of a sacrament in your Church. In the words of promise, spoken mutually between a man and woman, you show your face. But exactly what, Lord, did you bless at Cana? You blessed the permanent, exclusive union of one man and one woman, complementary beings, in a sacred bond that exists for the benefit of the partners and the procreation of children. I thank you, Lord, for going to that wedding; I thank you for the gift of your sacrament of Matrimony; and I pray for its defense against all who, though sometimes well-meaning, attempt to deface it through redefinition.

In the third and fourth of your Mysteries of Light, Lord Jesus, you proclaim the coming of your Kingdom and you promise glory to your servants. When you announced the advent of the Kingdom, you told of no arrival but your own. In the synagogue you taught that the prophecies of old had you as their subject. The ancient promises that prisoners would be set free, that the blind would see and the lame walk, that the hungry would be fed, were fulfilled in you. And so when you tell your disciples to pray, "Thy Kingdom come," you tell us to pray for your own reign in our hearts and in the thoughts, words, and deeds of all the world. You are the Kingdom. You rule the Kingdom. Inasmuch as I am a member of your Body and pattern my life on the unleavened bread of obedience, sincerity, and truth, I am in and of your Kingdom. Praised be God for His Kingdom of Light. Praised be Jesus, the light of the world.

Lord, you took your disciples up the mountain, and there you were transfigured before them. In that glorious, luminous event, you showed that the Son is above the law and the prophets; you prefigured your Resurrection from the dead; and you promised glory to your faithful followers. Grant, Lord Jesus, that I and all for whom I pray may come by your grace to that glory.

I see in the institution of the Eucharist, Lord Jesus, the culmination of your love and the promise of your sustaining presence in the Church and the world. Indeed, you are before me on the altar as a fulfillment of that promise. I pray that you, my Lord, who are the Sacrament of the Altar, may be the center of my life; and through me, that you will call those for whom I pray to you. Bread of heaven, be the light of my life. Feed me and grant that I may never be parted from you. Amen.

10. The Blessed Sacrament and the Sorrowful Mysteries

Worship of the Blessed Sacrament is worship of the Blessed Sacrifice.

My Lord, it is because of your sacrifice that you were able to triumph over death. It is because of your triumph over death that you are on the altar before me. Therefore, it is because of your sacrifice that you are here: made perfect through suffering, glorified by the Father.

That sacrifice began when you shed the glory of heaven and entered into your own creation. It continued through your life on earth, and was especially offered in the rejection you suffered from your own people. But it culminated in the terrible and beautiful events of Holy Thursday and Good Friday. For after the supreme light of the Institution of the Eucharist came the profound darkness of your betrayal, your rigged trial, and your execution. These events — the violence of sinful man against the Son of Man — are the Sorrowful Mysteries. And I, because of my sins, am responsible for them.

In Gethsemane your soul was sick with sorrow as you looked with disappointment upon the treatment you had received, and saw clearly the pain you were about to undergo. The first blood of your Passion came not from whip or nail but from your mental agony. How great your sorrow was. Then you were betrayed, tried, and scourged. In the scourging, even before being condemned, you bled through a thousand wounds. You enacted the low fate of a whipped slave, obedient even unto death.

What a mix of mockery and pain the crown of thorns was

— a concentrated image of the treatment you have received from your disobedient and rebellious servants. Including me. I pray, Lord Jesus, that I may never again depose you from your rightful reign in my life. I pray for your kingship over me and the whole human race. I pray that you will help me to wear whatever crown of rejection, ridicule, and pain you send me. And to know that when I do so, you are with me. Amen.

You, Lord — the Body before me on the altar — were weighted down with the awful freight of the cross. And now, two thousand years later, you have given me a very different web of circumstance in which to live. But in the elements of my life is a cross — often a bundle of many smaller crosses — that you call upon me to carry. Grant, my Lord, that I may lift and bear the cross you send me, and follow you. Thus may I become an offering to the Father in your name.

In the final Sorrowful Mystery, you were executed by crucifixion. A supremely painful death. A spectacle elevated for public viewing. You were lifted up like the Old Testament serpent. You were degraded like a biological specimen, a bug on a stick. You had no private death, but were the object of a thousand eyes, humiliated before man and crying "forsaken" before God.

But visible still in the darkness that covered the earth was the promise of divine mercy. Your Heart poured forth the water of cleansing and the blood of the New Covenant. You gave the Church your own Mother, giving us in turn to her in a marvelous adoption of grace. As you descended among the dead, you sent forth the means of eternal life to your people. Supremely sorrowful yet supremely promising, desperate yet hopeful, greatest good coming from the greatest malice: in your suffering and death is the promise of glory. Grant, Lord Jesus, that I may never aspire to resurrection without first embracing the sacrifice of your death. In that sacrifice lies all hope.

Reflections Before the Blessed Sacrament

    Mary, Mother of Sorrows, pray for me here before the Body of your Son, and for those for whom I pray. In accord with the will of your Firstborn, I take you as my Mother. I embrace your sorrow and pray for the joy of your help. Amen.

11. The Blessed Sacrament and the Glorious Mysteries

Jesus and Mary are together in glory. "Glory" often seems remote from us mere human beings, who are daily involved in the inglorious conflicts and struggles, irritations and distractions, of our lives. Often we forget who made us. Often we forget your presence, Lord. And yet St. Thérèse, our loving sister and holy friend in heaven, has taught us that you are especially present in the humble events of daily life; that in these events we can find you; that daily encounters provide intimations of the glory you have promised us. So I know that you are with me all the time, Lord, and wherever you are, glory truly awaits.

Your Mother, Mary, leads me to the hope of glory more surely than any other human being. After your Ascension into heaven, in company with the apostles, she knelt in your presence — as I do now. Hers was the humble lot of waiting, praying, hoping for your return. She continued to fulfill the vocation you had given her — to point to you and say, "Do whatever He tells you" (John 2:5), while, with the Church, she received your Body in Holy Communion.

The events of her own life had been anything but ordinary — including, as they did, giving birth to you, the Son of God, and caring for you as a child, then witnessing your ministry, sacrifice, and triumph over death. After your Ascension came the day-by-day life in the newborn Church, where Mary knelt before your priests to receive you in the Eucharist; where she cared for the needs of her fellow Christians, who are her children in you.

In heaven Mary still cares for her sons and daughters, with unmatched maternal solicitude. She came to this glory because she devoutly carried out all that you asked her to do. Called to your side in the Assumption, crowned Queen of Heaven by your hand, she dwells forever at the pinnacle of glory.

Though I am sinful, Lord, you promise me some measure of the glory that you have given your immaculate Mother. Surely she kneels with me here before you. Just as surely she sits enthroned beside you, next to you the brightest example and strongest advocate for our race. Lord Jesus, teach me the meaning of glory. May I always remember that glory in the present and glory to come depend entirely on my humble submission to your will. I cannot earn divine favor. I cannot by my own merit, of which I have none, be reconciled to the Father. I am wholly dependent on your merit. Grant that in the lowly tasks of daily life I may find you. Grant that, like Mary my Mother, I may trust in you for all things.

Her Glorious Mysteries began with your Resurrection from the dead. Lord, after you died on the cross you harrowed hell and conquered death. When you arose you brought mankind out of the shadow of mortality and into the light of your Resurrection. Because of that triumph over man's ancient enemy, I believe all that the Scriptures and the Church teach about you. In your Resurrection I see the clearest proof that I too will rise from the dead to share your glory.

When you ascended into heaven you took with you the hopes and aspirations of the whole human race. In the Holy of Holies you intercede for us. Bread of Heaven, resurrected Body of Christ before me on the altar, I offer you to the Father as my only plea. You, Lord, are my only Mediator and Advocate. May your holy Mother and all the saints, who kneel around your throne, share their spiritual goods with me.

O Holy Spirit of God, you who on Pentecost descended in fire on the apostles, grant that I may always follow your guidance.

Grant me, Lord Jesus, the gifts of your Holy Spirit: wisdom, understanding, counsel, fortitude, knowledge, piety, and fear of God. May I know and follow no other master.

Mother Mary, when Jesus called you to Himself in your glorious Assumption, an obscure daughter of Nazareth entered the Holy of Holies with our great High Priest. Mother of God, pray that I may truly become your child in all that I think, say, and do. Grant, Lord Jesus, that I may honor your Mother as you do. Blessed Virgin, before the resurrected Body of your Son I pray for your true reign in my life and all the life of the world. For your Heart, your Soul, and your Mind are wholly devoted to the interests of the Sacred Heart of Jesus. Queen of Heaven, pray for and with me here. Lord Jesus, bring me to the glory of heaven. Amen.

12. The Unleavened Bread of Sincerity and Truth

Lord Jesus, you spoke plainly at that Passover where you instituted the Holy Eucharist. You said, "Take this and eat it. This is my Body." At that moment the unleavened bread of the Passover was transformed — transubstantiated — into your true Body.

Of old, the Father had said that those who were protected by the blood of the Passover lamb would be safe from death. The final plague that Yahweh hurled against the stiff-necked Egyptians, the plague of death, was averted by the lamb's blood. Over those houses marked with the sacrifice the angel of death passed harmlessly.

Christ, our Passover, is sacrificed for us. We are marked with His Blood. Once He was dead, but now He lives forever. We live in His life, and He protects His own from death. Mark me, Lord Jesus, with your Blood. Feed me that I may live in the light of your Resurrection and share your life forever. May the sign of your sacrificial blood in my life keep me from the second death. Amen.

I know that leaven has two main senses in the Scriptures. First, it means malice, insincerity, untruth, uncleanness, dishonesty: the gas that inflates dough. "A little leaven leavens the whole lump." Yeast penetrates a piece of dough and causes it to swell. It weighs no more than before, it *is* no more than before, but it is puffed up so that the original flour seems to have increased. In this meaning of the leaven, leavened bread is an image for unreality, insincerity, dishonesty, even uncleanness. Those leavened with the old leaven are like counterfeit money. Fake. Thus the Pharisees in Judea exaggerated their holiness by dwelling on the minutiae of the law so that everyone could see their supposed righteousness. Thus have I also sometimes pretended to be better than I am; so have we all.

The new leaven, by contrast, is like the old *un*leaven. Knowing itself totally dependent upon God, it looks to you, Lord Jesus, for all its merit. Recognizing that self-aggrandizement and pretense lead to puffery without substance, the unleaven of honesty — the new leaven — strives to know the truth and live in freedom from all deception and illusion. St. Paul associated the old leaven with sins of the body, which seek the cover of darkness and twist one's understanding. The new leaven, by contrast, is life in the light, where dirt is removed and distortions disappear. It leads to deeper understanding of God and man.

Much that you teach me, Lord, is beyond my comprehension, and yet I believe because you are the Teacher. Your Resurrection attests to the reality of the general resurrection and of Judgment Day. It underscores the plain meaning of your words, "This is my Body." It guarantees the truth of your promise to be with your Church until the end. It brings the Church to reflect on the new leaven; to *become* the new leaven.

On Easter Sunday, you speak to us, Lord Jesus, through the words St. Paul wrote to the Christians at Corinth:

> Do you not know that a little yeast leavens all the dough? Clear out the old yeast, so that you may become a fresh batch of dough, inasmuch as you are unleavened. For our paschal lamb, Christ, has been sacrificed. Therefore, let us celebrate the feast, not with the old yeast, the yeast of malice and wickedness, but with the unleavened bread of sincerity and truth. (1 Corinthians 5:6-8)

Your sacrifice, Lord, is the Passover of the New Covenant.

Thus it is like the ancient Passover — a bridge between your Church and the law and prophets. The Easter baptismal water, blessed symbol of your death and resurrection, is our door to the glory won by your triumph over hell and the grave. We, born again in baptism, share in your passion and the victory you won. We new creatures, as St. Anselm teaches, celebrate your sacrifice with the unleavened bread of sincerity and truth. The leaven of our former malice is thrown out, and a new creature is filled and inebriated with the Lord Himself. For the effect of our sharing in the Body and Blood of Christ is to change us into what we receive.

Lord Jesus, Unleavened Bread of Heaven, I know that no secrets are hidden from you. You know my thoughts before I do, my words before they are formed. Make me a full participant in your sacrifice and Resurrection. Cleanse the thoughts of my heart and the words of my mouth. Remove from me the old leaven. May my deeds enact your will. May I become the true servant of your Kingdom to everyone I meet. Body and Soul, Blood and Divinity of Christ, make me true as you are true, unleavened as you are unleavened. Lord, make me a true member of your Body. Amen.

13. The Eucharist and the Sacrament of Penance

Mary, Mother of God, though you saw your Son crucified and then buried, though you saw Him ascend into heaven, you were never really separated from Him. Your hearts were joined always. He honored and cared for you always. And in the Eucharist He fed you always with the unleavened bread of sincerity and truth, until the time He called you to His side. Mother, I know that you are with me here, sharing your spiritual riches in the Communion of Saints. In adoring Him whom you adore, I join myself, by God's grace, with the worshiping choirs in heaven.

O Blessed Virgin, you join the Sacrament of Penance to this Saturday Devotion. You require Confession as a part of my offering. Bring me, Mother, to a wise understanding of this holy plan. Give me the integrity of this whole devotion.

Because I don't want to be separated from you, Lord Jesus, I confess my sins. Because I don't want ever again to disappoint you, Mother Mary — as I have often done — I seek Christ's face in the Sacrament of Penance. Because by my sins I have evicted you, Lord, from the throne of my heart and mind, I come to you, the fountain of mercy, and seek your forgiveness through your priest. This your holy Mother asks me to do.

Sin brings me disorder and sorrow. When I am in a state of unforgiven sin, I can't pray, I can't think right, my soul can't rest. My whole life is disturbed. At those times, Lord Jesus, I am separated from you. I am separated from receiving you in Holy Communion. For receiving Communion — or attempting Communion — when one is in a state of serious sin brings "harms and fears," and compounds the evil. At those times the conscience, the "original Vicar of Christ" (as Cardinal Newman calls the conscience) is hurt and disordered and will allow no peace. One piles sin upon sin when he shows by unworthy reception of the Eucharist that in practice he is actually willing to commit sacrilege. Grant that I may never be guilty of receiving Communion with a doubtful conscience.

Lord, have mercy on me, a sinner. Heart of Mary, pray for me.

How do I draw near again to Jesus? For the baptized, the Church teaches the cure for serious sin — recourse to Christ's mercy in the Sacrament of Confession. "As long as I would not speak, my bones wasted away," the psalmist writes; but when "I acknowledged my sin to you… you took away" my guilt (Psalm 32). Lord, I know you are present under the sign of bread before me. But you are no less present in the sacrament of healing, which I seek as I offer this Saturday Devotion to you. Thus your holy Mother taught at Fatima. Show me your face, Lord Jesus, in the face of your priest and in the words of absolution.

As you were wounded for the sins of mankind, you bore innumerable cuts. As by your stripes we are made whole, you suffered innumerable blows. For the sins of the world are so numerous and grave that they can be expiated only by an infinite Atonement — such as you alone can offer. You call me to that atonement. The Sacrament of Confession is the doorway to worthy reception of the Eucharist. Holy Sacrament of the Altar, resurrected Body of the crucified Son of God, I hunger to receive you worthily.

Let the words of King David, spiritually devastated by the self-inflicted wounds of sin, be my words:

> Cleanse me of sin with hyssop, that I may be purified;
> wash me, and I shall be whiter than snow.…

> Turn away your face from my sins,
> and blot out all my guilt....
> Cast me not out from your presence,
> and take not your Holy Spirit from me (Psalm 51).

Soul of Christ, never let me be separated from you again.

Confession

The Sacrament of Confession is also called the Sacrament of Penance or the Sacrament of Reconciliation. The Blessed Mother asks us to receive this sacrament as part of our First Saturday Devotion. In so doing, we ally ourselves with the holy men and women of every age who have recognized their need of repentance and forgiveness. We acknowledge God as our Redeemer, who wants to recreate His image in us. And we prepare ourselves to receive Jesus in Holy Communion.

Why Do Penance?

Mary and the Sacrament of Penance. On this First Saturday I offer reparation to the Immaculate Heart of Mary. I visit the Blessed Sacrament with her. I reflect on the Eucharist and on the mysteries of the life of Christ. Today I publicly recite at least five decades of the Rosary. At Holy Mass today I receive Jesus in Holy Communion. But rich though these gifts are, I know they are not all. Our Lady of Fatima also asks that the Sacrament of Penance or Confession be a part of the First Saturday Devotion. Why?

It seems that the whole purpose of the First Saturday Devotion is to draw closer to Mary, and through her to Jesus. All the holy deeds and prayers of the saints, by the grace of the sacrifice of Christ, form a great treasury of merit in which I can share. This sharing is known as the Communion of Saints, and Mary is the greatest figure in it. The Blessed Virgin's merits are so far above those of the other saints that she is rightly called their Queen. Around her are gathered her children, Christ's faithful disciples. With her they pray. Gathered together in the Communion of Saints, the holy men and women of every era of salvation history have great spiritual goods that they can share with me even now. It is those goods that I want. It is that communion that I want to cultivate and enhance. Through the holy means at my disposal, I want to draw closer to those who in Christ have won victory over sin and death.

But I am completely unworthy of so great and holy a company. I see with pain how often I have disappointed the Blessed Mother and thwarted her hopes for me: how often I have given in to temptation and actually welcomed the fleeting pleasure of sin. How unworthy I have become, how unfit for saintly company. My conscience *convicts* me of grievous wrong. The result is clear. The first effect of my guilt, as Venerable John Henry Newman says, is to "burden and sadden" my mind. In that sad state of thought, I recognize that I have separated myself from God. A heavy, an unbearable, recognition. But Mary asks me to leave this weight behind, so as to draw closer to her and to her Firstborn Son. She asks me to do so in a sacramental confession.

I also see that penance — sorrow for sin, confession, and reparation — is at the heart of the message that Mary brought at Fatima. Penance is powerful. It can even change the course of history — can bring about the conversion of whole nations that have rebelled against God. With Christ's help, it can also bring about my own transformation. I want to be remade in the image of Christ. I want to be among His saints, who have put aside all weights so as to ascend to His presence. Confession will bring a change that I earnestly seek.

But the goodness of confession extends beyond me. Purification before prayer also helps me to fulfill a mission to others given me by Mary. At Fatima, Our Lady lamented the fact that many souls are lost because no one prays for them. These poor rebels against God arrive at the bar of judgment without a prayer — unless I pray for them. Our Lady says that many of them fall down into hell because no one prays on their behalf. Because Mary expressed her love for them at Fatima, I will pray for them. I will do penance for my own sins so that I may plead with a pure heart for the dying sinners whose loss so pains the Blessed Virgin.

Before confession I will examine my conscience. As I do so, I will try to understand the gravity of my own sins. I will let Christ shine His light on me, for His Passion made possible my forgiveness. His sacrifice — His faithfulness and mercy — shines a bright light on my rebellion and weakness. This light is like the surgeon's light, in which my corruption is clearly visible. But under this light I can be cleansed, for Jesus has borne the cost of my forgiveness. As St. Peter teaches, by Christ's wounds I am healed (cf. 1 Peter 2:24). By the merit of His Passion I am reconciled with the Father. Thus my soul, moved to penance by Christ's suffering, as the *Catechism of the Council of Trent* taught, will be fortified and invigorated by His love. So cleansed and strengthened, I will enter into His presence in the company of His holy Mother, and there plead for the conversion of sinners as she asked. May God grant that through my prayers some of them may be saved.

I must try to make a good confession — honest, extenuating nothing, self-critical. Is mine a confession of necessity, brought about by mortal sin? Must I receive sacramental absolution before going to Communion? Or is mine a confession of devotion, made not because of current guilt for great evildoing but in order to strengthen an already healthy union with Christ and His saints? Whatever the answer, as I examine my conscience, I will not minimize my sins. St. Dorotheus rightly teaches that "if someone examines himself carefully and with fear of God, he will never find himself completely innocent." And so it is. I am certainly not innocent. May the Almighty Father grant me the salutary fear of God that is a gift of the Holy Spirit. May I never forget that, even though I may not have committed grave sin since my last confession, I have nevertheless often enough separated myself from God, willfully and shamefully. *May God grant me the grace of a good confession.*

Prayer: Lord Jesus, you know all things. What folly it would be for me to pretend before you, from whom no secrets are hidden, to whom no lies can be told. What sacrilege it would be for me to make an incomplete or dishonest confession. Grant me total honesty as I examine myself in preparation for receiving your Sacrament of Penance. Grant me the grace to know my sins, to confess them to you in the person of your priest, and to do not only the light penance that he will require but additional acts of reparation to your Sacred Heart and to the Immaculate Heart of Mary. Lord, please forgive me my sins. I am so sorry for them. Hear my prayers and then have mercy also on those for whom I pray. Look with favor on all my other intentions, purified by the bounty of your mercy. Mary, Mother, be with me and help me. Amen.

Note

The teaching of the Blessed Virgin at Fatima allows us to receive the Sacrament of Penance within eight days before or after the First Saturday itself. Just as at any other time, however, no one who is conscious of having committed a serious sin should receive the First Saturday Communion without first going to confession.

On Conscience and the Commandments

What is the relationship between the Ten Commandments and one's conscience? Why is the Decalogue — the Ten Commandments — traditionally used as a framework for the examination of conscience? The answer must be that the law of God forms the *content* of a well-formed conscience. Otherwise it would make no sense to examine our consciences by asking if we have stolen, lied, committed adultery, etc., for these sins would be irrelevant to our consciences. A conscience without specified content is a free-floating permission machine. A conscience that isn't filled with the teachings of the Church leads only to the spiritually dead condition of those who sin without worry.

And that is in fact the sad state of many consciences now. False teaching on conscience has flourished in the modern world, both in and outside the Church. The key to that false teaching, especially in the Church, is this: People observe that it is always wrong to violate one's conscience, but then they draw the false conclusion that an unaided conscience is a reliable guide to conduct. That is, they note the necessary role of conscience in making moral decisions, and then conclude that whatever they want to do is all right as long as it doesn't violate their consciences. Never mind, they say, *what* your conscience tells you, as long as you don't violate it. Such people are exemplars of *solipsism*, the false philosophical and moral belief that right and wrong are determined by subjectively held opinion.

But this is not the teaching of Christ and of the Sacred Tradition of the Church. Sure, the Church teaches that everyone has a conscience. Everyone has an authoritative internal voice that approves or disapproves of thoughts, words, and deeds that one may choose. The Church also teaches, however, that the conscience may be malformed; that in order to be formed properly, the conscience must be formed in accord with the teaching of Christ.

Here is a modern analogy: The conscience is like computer hardware. We must add the right software — or content — in order for the conscience to function properly. What we feed the computer is important. A bad input will cause a bad output. You probably know the acronym GIGO, which stands for "Garbage In, Garbage Out." Consciences can be filled with error. How else, for instance, could seemingly well-intentioned individuals murder millions of people in the name of God with the goal of establishing a so-called ideal society and feel no sense of guilt?

For another analogy, the faculty of conscience is like a bookshelf. We must carefully choose what books to put in it. And the Holy Spirit, through the Church's teaching, is our guide.

Some examinations of conscience use the Sermon on the Mount, especially the Beatitudes, as their outline. This is right and good. For Jesus taught the Ten Commandments, of which He was the actual author, and then He added to them. Thus He not only reiterated the Ten Commandments, He deepened them and spiritualized them. The beatitude that praises the "poor in spirit," for instance, may be seen as a deeper version of the commandment not to murder. Why? The poor in spirit are humbly disposed toward God, and consequently less likely to vent murderous anger on their fellow man. The poor in spirit recognize that they are dependent upon God, not only for their daily necessities, but for their very existence. Consequently, they are less likely to demand perfection from others and judge its lack with anger and murder.

Confession

In short, though this book uses the Ten Commandments as its framework for an examination of conscience, the reader should understand that these commandments form a significant part of the teaching of Jesus, who understood them profoundly, taught them in all their spiritual depth, and willed that His Church follow them. After all, He gave them to Moses at Mount Sinai.

How to Confess

First, before you go to confession, examine your conscience. Do so honestly, with a real understanding of the seriousness of your sin. The following sections are designed to help you do this. Some other guide to examination of conscience may, of course, be as good. Most are shorter. But don't skip the self-examination. Don't just go to confession without previous self-criticism. After you have meditated on the precise thoughts, words, and deeds that have wounded your conscience, you are ready for confession.

When you get to the priest, you often have the option of confessing face-to-face with him or from behind a screen designed to preserve your anonymity. The choice is completely yours. If you feel comfortable sitting in the presence of your confessor and telling him your most intimate secrets, then do so. This mode of confession was made available after the Second Vatican Council. If you prefer the more traditional posture of kneeling behind a screen that hides you from the priest's vision, then choose that.

Whichever manner of confession you prefer, you should remember that your confession is totally private. Priests are obligated under oath to keep what you say secret. They have sworn actually to submit to death rather than to reveal what you say — or even if you say anything. So speak confidently. But also speak softly, remembering that others in line to confess have no desire or right to hear you. *You should also remember that the priest is not hearing you in his own person, but in the person of Christ.* Though a clergyman is listening to you, he represents Jesus. The priest is there as a conduit of the sacramental presence of Christ.

Traditionally, confession begins with the penitent's saying, "Bless me, Father, for I have sinned." Some recent guides say to make the sign of the cross and say "In the name of the Father, the Son, and the Holy Spirit."

The priest's initial response may be "Yes" or "Go ahead." If you have asked for a blessing, he may say something like "May the Lord grant you the grace of a good confession" or "May the Lord be in your heart and on your lips that you may worthily confess your sins." After the priest's opening words,

- tell him how long it has been since your last confession. If this is your first confession, say so. If you haven't been to confession for years, don't be ashamed to say so. There are many others like you. Then,
- tell him your sins.

Don't spare yourself. We all want to minimize or deny our own wrongdoing. We are prone to say that what we have done "is not so bad." But when we reflect that the *least* of our sins, even venial ones, require the blood of Christ for their expiation, we start to see our wrongdoing in the proper light. The Sacrament of Reconciliation is a necessity in the case of mortal sin. Though it is not a necessity in the case of "small" sins, there is no sin too small to confess. This fact emphasizes that we are fallen and in need of Christ's redemption, no matter how well we have been behaving recently.

Don't use euphemisms. Call your sins by their right names. Euphemisms — nice words designed to smooth over a rough reality — are actually a form of lie. They are always intended to minimize some unattractive truth. In pushing for legalized abortion, for instance, the death peddlers referred to unborn babies as "fetal material" or "a blob of cells." Nothing wrong with removing a wart, is there? The murder was called "terminating a pregnancy." These lies made killing the baby easier. An analogy: If you have committed adultery, don't say that you have "behaved improperly." Remember who you are talking to. Trying to make your sins sound nice to Jesus is foolish. Call the act what it is.

The priest may question you or make comments as you proceed. When he does so, remember that he is speaking for Jesus and the Church. At the end of your confession, make some concluding statement such as "Though I no doubt have committed many more sins, these are the ones that have been troubling me and that brought me here today." Then listen to the priest. He may make suggestions about how to overcome your sins, he may ask questions about what you have said, or he may move directly to the end of the sacrament.

The last part of your confession is an "Act of Contrition." This is a prayer that expresses your sorrow for your sins. Though some priests let you omit it in the confessional, expecting that you will make such an act outside the confessional, they probably should not do so. Sorrow for sins is necessary before forgiveness can occur and should be specifically expressed. Though our sorrow is never deep or sincere enough, we must make an effort to reject our sinful behavior. The act of contrition is evidence that we have tried, and that we are willing to change. It should not be skipped.

Here is an act of contrition that includes references to both imperfect and perfect contrition. *Imperfect contrition* arises from fear of punishment. Unforgiven sin leads to spiritual death — an eternity in hell. Fear of that death is sufficient to gain forgiveness. But it is still imperfect. *Perfect contrition*, however, comes not from self-interest or fear of punishment, but from the knowledge that God is worthy of our complete devotion, and that sin is not only evil and deadly but monumentally inappropriate.

An Act of Contrition

O my God, I am sorry for my sins, and I hate them because I fear the loss of heaven and the pains of hell, but most of all because by them I offend you who are all good and worthy of all my love. I firmly resolve with the help of your grace to do penance and to amend my life. Amen.

After the Act of Contrition, the priest will give you a penance to perform. Three acts of the confessing sinner — repentance, confession, and acceptance of the prescribed penance — are essential for the sacrament to be valid, except in unusual cases such as when an unconscious person in danger of death receives absolution. Invariably, the penance is light. It usually involves saying a few prayers or doing some good deed or meditating on some aspect of God's grace. Though at various times in the Church's history extremely harsh penances have been exacted — some of them lasting for decades — the Church now recognizes the validity of easily accomplished penances. This recognition is in line with the understanding that forgiveness is a free gift of God; it cannot be earned, even by a lifetime of self-denial. And so the penance is a *symbolic* offering to the Father that expresses our intention to offer ourselves completely to His service, and to accept the grace of His forgiveness, which comes to us in spite of our unworthiness.

It is always a good idea to resolve to do more penance than the priest requires. By the grace of God, our extra offerings have merit, for He receives them in Christ's name.

After prescribing your penance, the priest will give you absolution. The formula for absolution begins with a summary statement of how God gives power to His Church to impart the forgiveness of Christ to the penitent sinner. Then follow the words, "I absolve you from your sins in the name of the Father, and of the Son, and of the Holy Spirit." This verbal formula is the sign of the sacramental presence of Christ. Just as water is the sign of spiritual cleansing in baptism, the priest's words of forgiveness are the sign of the sacrament of Penance or Reconciliation. Like all the Church's sacraments, this sign actually gives the grace of which it speaks. From it we receive *Christ's* forgiveness.

After the absolution, the priest will dismiss you. He may say something like "Go in peace," to which a proper response is "Thanks be to God." Another frequent dismissal is "Give thanks to the Lord, for He is good." To which the response is, "His mercy endures forever."

Whatever the priest's dismissal is, your next step is to do your penance. If it is prayers, say them in the presence of the Blessed Sacrament before you leave the church. Otherwise, do as the priest has specified. You should remember that if you leave the confessional intending to do your penance and later forget to do it, no sin is committed and no guilt incurred. But the possibility of forgetting is another reason to do your penance *as soon as possible*. Forgetting to do one's penance is not much of a sign of gratitude.

Examination of Conscience in Light of the Ten Commandments

Note: Meditation on all the commandments is far too big a job for a single visit to church. But the Ten Commandments are also too important to slight. Therefore, it may be best to break the process down into manageable parts. The discussion of each commandment in the following section begins with an explanation of the meaning of the commandment and continues with a series of self-directed questions. To make the whole examination manageable, a reader might meditate on one of the commandments each Saturday — read the explanation of it, think of its meaning and apply it to his or her life — and then read just the questions for the other commandments. Then on the next First Saturday, another commandment can be studied in depth.

Commandment 1
I am the Lord, your God.
You shall not have strange gods before me.

The first requirement of this commandment is to remember who God is — to remember that *He* is the "I" of the commandment, and not anything or anyone else. God exists and is the source of existence. Nothing can be elevated into His place. Anything that absorbs my attention so that I forget my Creator is an idol.

The second requirement is to know myself as a created being, and to know that all beings, animate and inanimate, are God's creation.

I should never forget these profound truths as I go about my daily life. I must never forget that my whole life, including my innermost thoughts, takes place in the immediate presence of the God who created me. When I do forget — when I act as if God did not exist, or as if I were not accountable to Him — I interrupt His reign over me. I negate the petition in the *Lord's Prayer* "Thy Kingdom come." I make an idol of whatever so engages me.

God made me, I am His. The fact that I am a creature, sustained in being by my Creator, makes all the difference in my life. It means that I have nothing that I wasn't given. It means that I owe all that I am and have to Him who made me and holds me up, who gives me every breath I take, who grants every beat of my heart.

The second clause of the First Commandment tells me that I must not put anything ahead of my duty to my Creator. Everything besides God is His creation. All entities are His creatures. No creature deserves, or should receive, the honor that is due to God alone.

Examination of Conscience in Light of the Ten Commandments

The First Commandment is the overriding commandment because God's existence and His revelation of what is right and wrong stand behind every other command. Whenever I break one of the commandments — as I have often done — I first reject God's direction of my life. I kick Him out of my heart, at least temporarily, and take the rule of myself away from Him. I say, in effect, "My will — not Thine — be done." If, for instance, I have stolen, if I have lied, if I have burned with lust, if I have skipped Mass, if I have desired someone else's possessions: in any sin that I have committed, I have first raised my own will above God's. In so doing, I have broken the First Commandment as I went about breaking one of the other commandments. This is the teaching of Sacred Tradition. The *Catechism of the Council of Trent* says that the punishment for breaking the First Commandment is "attached to all the other Commandments."

To consider my own talents and intellect sufficient for the needs of life is to break the First Commandment by means of the first deadly sin, pride. That poison leads to all kinds of sin and misery. On the other hand, when I strive to submit my will to the reign of God, I live in faith, hope, and charity. Faith is knowledge of God's rule. Hope is the joyful acceptance of His promises, the trust that He will never betray those who seek to know and serve Him. Such faith and hope lead to a life in which charity, the love that comes from God and is properly returned to Him, overflows into a love for my human neighbors. To abjure pride by knowing that I am a completely dependent being, and to live in faith, hope, and love: this is obedience to the First Commandment.

Have I kept the First Commandment?

1. Have I lived in faith? Have I rejected the sovereignty of God by denying or doubting His existence? Have I rejected His rule by denying any teaching of the Church? Have I thus made myself an idol? Have I made an idol of some activity?
2. Have I lived in hope? Have I given room to despair, the first negation of hope, in my heart? Have I tempted God by presumption, the second negation of hope? That is: Have I presumed that God's judgment does not apply to me, that I will always be in His grace no matter what I do? Have I thus made void the promise of God's judgment?
3. Have I professed love of God while scorning or hating my fellow man? Have I refused to be moved by the plight of those who are truly poor, the least of Christ's brothers? Have I given what I could give to alleviate suffering? Have I forgotten that God has given me all that I have?
4. Have I sunk to such a level as to seek supernatural knowledge or help from magic or astrology? Have I given credence to superstitions? Have I assumed that God's favor can be forced through recitation of magic formulas or enactment of magic ceremonies? Have I treated God like some sort of supernatural vending machine — made to work by a magical formula or ceremony — rather than the totally free and gracious Creator, the source of all being?
5. Have I separated my public witness — at work, in politics, or elsewhere — from what I profess to believe? Do I profess belief in God and yet deny that belief by my actions? Do I vote for pro-abortion candidates? Do I approve of the effort to bring good from evil — for instance, to produce cures for illnesses by the destruction of human embryos — thus denying the teaching of Christ's Church? Do I stand up for

the truth whenever possible? Have I joined or supported organizations or religious communions that are hostile to the Catholic Church? Do my neighbors know that I am Catholic, and that the Church makes a difference in my life? Or have I kept my light hidden?
6. Do I fail to cultivate my faith? Do I avoid occasions of sin, or do I relish them? Do I watch television shows filled with sexual immorality, or movies of the same kind? Do I read pornographic texts or look at pornographic pictures? On the other hand, do I pray regularly? Do I ask God to enlarge my faith, hope, and love? Do I strive truly to love the Lord with all my heart, mind, and soul, as the Gospel bids me? Do I seek and pray for true repentance, true cleanness of heart?
7. In all that I think, say, or do, do I strive to let the Eternal Father rule my life?

Commandment 2
You shall not take the name of the Lord your God in vain.

A personal being is inseparable from his name. As God is the Supreme Personal Being, and the author of all existence, He is inseparable from all the names by which man refers to Him. Any attribute of God — omnipotence, immortality, omniscience, holiness — can be used to name Him. We call God the Holy One of Israel and the Holy Immortal One, for instance. Or simply "God." No matter what name we use, when we refer to God, we must do so reverently.

The Second Commandment grows immediately out of the First. The First Commandment tells me who God is: my Creator and Sustainer, to whom I owe my existence and well-being. The Second Commandment teaches me to revere my Creator under all His names.

Just how far Western culture has declined from reverence toward God's name is reflected in much of the language that we hear on the street and in the media. The phenomenon of a "shock jock," a radio personality whose main selling point is the shock value of his language, would have been impossible in previous ages. The seriousness has also been drained out of ordinary language that implies God's presence. For example, in flippant journalistic use every intention, no matter how unimportant, is now called a "vow." But we servants of God know that real vows are more solemn and more thoughtfully grounded than that. The word "vow" refers to God.

We should be aware of the origins of the words we use. Some popular expressions, present and past, will not pass examination under the Second Commandment. "Dadgum," for instance, comes from an obvious enough profanity. The kids' word "Gadzooks" comes from the phrase "God's hooks," i.e., the nails that pierced Christ's hands and feet. We should be circumspect in our use of references to blood, for the Blood of Christ is often profanely alluded to. In all our language, we should be thoughtful and reverent; we should remember that even if no one who hears us is offended at what we say — or even if no one hears us — our language reflects our spiritual condition. True faith in God issues in reverent language about Him. It is true that such expressions as "Dadgum" or "Gosh" are euphemistic ways of making asseverations. They are not often meant seriously. But it is still good to know that they express a desire to curse without cursing, and to remember that the Lord Jesus promises we will be held accountable for "every idle word" we say.

Like all the commandments, the Second Commandment holds me to both negative and positive obedience. Negatively, any

Examination of Conscience in Light of the Ten Commandments

profanation of God or that which belongs to Him is forbidden. Positively, in public and private I must strive to honor God's name. We pray in the *Our Father* at every Mass and in every Rosary, "Hallowed be Thy name." We are responsible for this hallowing. We are responsible for the holy treatment of God's name. The Church teaches that when her sons and daughters publicly profess their faith before the world, they fulfill this command. We honor the name of God by letting our faith be known, by respecting Scripture, by offering all our thoughts, words, and deeds to the Father in the name of the Son, by having our children baptized in the name of the Holy Trinity, and by many other affirmations of the Faith.

On the other hand, we *dis*honor the name of God when we take it in vain, when we swear false or evil oaths, when we invoke the Holy Name for a trivial or unholy purpose, when we curse people, or when we ridicule devout people or distance ourselves from them. When we support pro-abortion politicians, especially those who claim to be Catholic, do we not say by our actions that God's name and His teaching in the Church are unimportant to us?

Have I kept the Second Commandment?

1. Have I cursed? Have I used the name of God merely to exhibit anger? Have I used the name of God for mere verbal emphasis?
2. Have I invoked God's name for any unworthy reason?
3. Have I unworthily or vainly used the name of the Blessed Virgin Mary or of one of God's lesser saints?
4. Have I broken a vow to do something good — e.g., to keep my marriage promises faithfully? Have I thus dishonored the auspices — the name — under which my marriage was contracted?

5. Have I vowed to do something evil, thus perverting the name of God?
6. Have I sworn falsely, thus calling God to witness to a lie?
7. Have I failed to profess my faith in Christ in order to avoid embarrassment or some other form of persecution? Have I been ashamed of His Name? Do I not know that if I deny Him before men, He will deny me before His Father?

Commandment 3

Remember the sabbath day to keep it holy. Six days you shall labor and do all your work; but the seventh day is a sabbath to the Lord your God; in it you shall not do any work.

It is *natural* to want to give formal thanks to the Creator, for He has given us all that we have, including our own existence. The requirement for some kind of ceremonial gratitude is therefore an outgrowth of the natural law. That this gratitude should be expressed through the devotion of a "sabbath" day and a series of memorial days is, however, a part of the *positive* law, over and above the natural law. Though all the commandments pertain one way or another to the natural law, the Third stands out by specifying aspects of the positive law. Still, these ceremonial requirements come from God, just like the moral requirements. Unlike, for instance, traffic laws, the requirements of the Third Commandment are divine as well as positive.

Under the guidance of the Holy Spirit, the Church decided very early in her history to celebrate the Holy Sacrifice of the Mass on Sunday. In addition to making Him literally present, this wonderful rite incorporates a formal memorial of the Lord's sacrifice

Examination of Conscience in Light of the Ten Commandments

and of His Resurrection. Why Sunday? Wouldn't Thursday be appropriate, since it was on a Thursday that the Mass was instituted? Under the guidance of the Holy Spirit, the Church wanted to memorialize the entire Paschal event, including its glorious later chapters. Though the Mass began on Holy Thursday, the Resurrection occurred on Sunday, the Church was established on Sunday, and the first Christians met on Sunday "to break bread" in the Eucharist. And so Sunday became our *Sabbath*, the day to which the Third Commandment applies in the Church. In time, Holy Church added other principal obligatory feasts pertaining to Our Lord and to His Mother. But throughout the Church year, Sunday is the dominant holy day of obligation. As a result of the Church's divinely guided decisions, all Catholics have a solemn duty to be present at Mass *on Sundays and all other holy days of obligation*, unless prevented by a serious reason; and to abstain from all unnecessary work on these days.

How real is this obligation? Why can I not "commune with God" by sleeping late or playing golf or fishing? The answer is that any deliberate breach of one of the Ten Commandments is seriously sinful; if I, as a Catholic, deliberately choose such disobedience, I commit a mortal sin. So failure to keep the Sabbath is gravely sinful. Catholics are required to attend Mass unless truly impeded. As a Catholic, I should go out of my way to fulfill this obligation, even when on vacation. I should also make a genuine effort to avoid working for pay on Sunday. Sunday is to be a day of rest and reflection.

My Mass obligation is clear enough. What about the work requirement? How can I survive in our thoroughly secular society if I can't work on Sunday? The Church's definition of "necessary work" has broadened considerably: it now includes not only such jobs as nursing, which know no day of rest. It now also acknowledges the secular business culture in which we live, a culture in which Sunday work is often required of all ordinary employees. If I *must* work on Sunday in order to have a job and feed my family, then that work is not sinful. But looking for *extra* work on Sunday would be sinful unless my financial condition really required it. Sunday work does not in itself excuse me from Mass. If I must work on Sunday, I still have to make a sincere effort to fulfill my Sabbath obligation. The Church makes the Saturday vigil Mass available for this need. Wherever I am on Sunday — even at work — I must sanctify the day by prayer and reflection on God, on my need of Him, and on the story of salvation. Unpaid work — charity, doing the works of mercy — is very appropriate for Sunday.

The Third Commandment goes further. It urges you and me to think of the whole revolving year in terms of salvation history. We not only attend Mass each Sunday, but make the passage of all our time meaningful by offering it to God. We punctuate the year with thoughtful, holy celebrations of our faith — from Advent to Christmas to the Easter season, in all the memorials of the saints, in the daily spiritual bread of Ordinary Time. The Third Commandment might be called the "Calendar Commandment," since it bids the faithful to refresh their minds regularly with reflection on the chief events in the life of Christ and of the Church. As we Catholics mark the Church year, our understanding of the events of salvation history is renewed and deepened annually. These events become even more important to us than the secular observances that may fall on the same days. For the devout, January 1, for instance, is the solemnity of the Mother of God — and only secondarily New Year's Day.

Have I kept the Third Commandment?

1. Have I missed Mass on Sunday or a holy day of obligation when I didn't have to?
2. Do I do unnecessary work on Sunday?

3. Where in my scale of importance does the remembrance of my salvation fall? Do I acknowledge Sundays and holy days of obligation as my most important "calendar commitments," or do I ignore God by skipping them?
4. Do I allow God to sanctify each of my days by offering my thoughts, words, and actions to Him in the name of Jesus and in union with Mary's prayers?
5. Do I reject God's ownership of most of my time and consider it "my own," or do I acknowledge His sovereignty and think of all times and places as belonging to Him?

COMMANDMENT 4

Honor your father and your mother, that you may live long upon the land that the Lord your God will give you.

The Fourth Commandment is about family obligations. The Church, however, extends the meaning of this commandment to obligations relating to all legitimate human authority. Just as the first three commandments regulate human relations with God, the fourth and subsequent commandments regulate our relations with each other. The fourth tells where honor and respect are due. The following commandments forbid specific immoral and antisocial actions.

First, the family. As children we are obligated to obey our mother and father. As adult children, though we no longer owe obedience to our parents, we still owe respect and honor to them. We are obliged to consult with them about the conduct of our lives, to respect their wishes as far as possible, and to be kind and considerate toward them. Is there any generation that has not considered itself wiser than its parents? Isn't there always a temptation to avoid them? Modern society holds a particular danger here. Nursing homes have multiplied. The extended family has diminished in importance. Now, more and more people are tempted to get rid of their parents by institutionalizing them. Though nursing homes have their legitimate place, the best place for aging parents — a place *owed* to them by their children — is in the home. If possible, we should take care of our parents ourselves. The Scriptures assure us that such care is a valuable offering to God.

Parents also have natural obligations to their children, especially obligations to raise them in the Faith. The Church teaches in the writings of Vatican II that parents are the "first and best" teachers of their children. Which means that parents have a more important role than the Church or school in training their children to love and serve God, and to love their neighbors as themselves.

Childhood respect for parents reflects the duty that we all have toward God. We must all strive to be obedient and respectful children of our heavenly Father. This naturally means that we should obey the moral law and accept the teachings of the Church in matters of faith and morals. It also means that we should maintain a loving, trusting attitude toward our Creator and Savior. Strangely enough, spiritual childhood is necessary for *maturity* in Christ. An adult Christian is a child before God. Jesus taught that we must "become as little children" before we can "enter the kingdom of God." The psalmist writes that his soul is "stilled and quieted" like a little child in his mother's lap. This state of mind is often hard to achieve, especially in times of trial. We complain against God when someone we love dies, when natural disaster strikes, when poverty or disease overtakes us, when anything bad happens. We think that we can hardly stand it. We may even accuse God of unjustly betraying us. But Jesus — we must remember — took upon Himself the pain of bereavement, of rejection, of temptation, of torture and death. Though we may not understand what has happened to us, though we may be crushed with grief, we are not alone, for the Savior "bears in His heart all wounds" (as a Catholic poet, Edith Sitwell, wrote).

No example of spiritual childhood surpasses that of the Holy Family. Although Joseph was clearly the head of the family, he devoted his life to Mary and the infant Jesus. He perfectly followed the divine rule for husbands to which St. Paul later gave voice: "Husbands, love your wives" (Ephesians 5:25). When Mary was carrying the Lord in her womb, Joseph turned to God for guidance and obediently accepted the Lord's directions. At the risk of social ostracism, even at the risk of death, Joseph took upon himself the high calling of caring for the Virgin and Child, in humble obedience to God the Father. In accord with the Fourth Commandment, Jesus Himself — though He was the author of all the commandments — was obedient to Joseph and Mary. Mary answered St. Gabriel's announcement of the Incarnation with perfect submission: "Let it be done to me according to your word" (Luke 1:38). When Jesus was a man and ready to begin His public ministry, Mary acknowledged His divinity and authority: "Do whatever He tells you" (John 2:5). The Holy Family is thus a perfect embodiment of the spiritual childhood that constitutes true maturity in the service of God, and therefore a perfect example of obedience to the Fourth Commandment. In fact, we would do well to meditate on *all* the commandments as Jesus, Mary, and Joseph lived them out.

The Church extends the meaning of the Fourth Commandment beyond the family, however. She also teaches that this commandment requires respect for all legitimate authority. This includes the law, courts, civil officers, employers, teachers, and anyone else who holds lawful authority in some sphere of our lives.

But the requirement to obey secular and civil law is not absolute. The one qualification that applies to all exercise of authority is this: We must obey God rather than men. So when a human being orders us to do something immoral, or when a human law authorizes an objective evil such as abortion, our duty of obedience is canceled. In fact, we are obliged to *dis*obey. If civil authorities uphold evil, we are obliged to disrespect those authorities.

Have I kept the Fourth Commandment?

1. Have I disrespected my parents or dishonored them? Have I failed to take care of them in their old age? Have I failed to consider the respect that I owe them?
2. Have I failed to respect my children as persons created in the image of God? Have I set a bad example for them? Have I failed to teach them the Faith? Do I practice the Faith myself as a model for them? Have I nagged them so as to lead them to lose heart?
3. Have I failed to respect the dignity and authority of those persons whom God has given responsibility for civil society?
4. Have I dishonored my social responsibilities by committing some serious crime? Do I owe someone, or society, retribution?

COMMANDMENT 5
You shall not kill.

In the teaching of the Church, the meaning of the Fifth Commandment goes far beyond its literal sense. For instance, Jesus adds His own teaching about *anger* to the Fifth Commandment. He says that deliberate anger is a type of mental murder, so anger is closely related to killing. Following Him in her theological reflection, the Church extends the commandment to all kinds of unnecessary violence between persons: not only literal violence, but also violent attitudes. It's not going too far to say that even an unforgiving attitude — which is, after all, the opposite of praying for your enemies — is forbidden by the Fifth Commandment. If I go around with a chip on my shoulder, always ready to react to others with hostility, I am breaking the Fifth Commandment whether I kill or even attack anyone or not.

But in spite of its breadth of application, the Fifth Commandment is also limited. Even in Old Testament times, the word *kill* in this commandment was interpreted to mean "murder." It meant killing the *innocent*. It did not include capital punishment or killing combatants in a justified war. In the Old Testament the extensive use of the death penalty for serious crimes, as well as the right to kill enemies of Israel in combat and afterward, was never denied.

These features of the Fifth Commandment are also a part of the Church's constant teaching. Capital punishment for certain crimes is not only allowed; the *Catechism of the Catholic Church* (#2266) teaches as well-founded "the right and duty of legitimate public authority to punish malefactors by means of penalties commensurate with the gravity of the crime, not excluding, in cases of extreme gravity, the death penalty." The Council of Trent teaches that the execution of those who have committed heinous crimes actually *fulfills* the Fifth Commandment. So it would seem that the Church has no real tradition of radical pacifism. Sacred Tradition does not demand the abolition of capital punishment, nor does it teach that all war is wrong. Far from it, it teaches that some crimes are truly capital and that some wars are justified. When a war is justified, it may actually be morally required.

The Fifth Commandment also does not include accidental killing and killing in self-defense, both of which, though terrible, are morally blameless. But it *does* include accidental killing that is the result of an evil act. A robber who "accidentally" kills a bank teller is guilty of murder.

There is a clear distinction in Church teaching between individuals and governments. The Fifth Commandment is broken by *individual* actions, or actions taken by groups that have no legitimate government function. The government ought to punish, even execute, some criminals. But I sin against the Fifth Commandment if I take the punishment of a criminal into my own hands. I sin even more grievously if I attack or kill an innocent person.

Which brings us to the most horrendous mass murder of our time. In this country, we have murdered more than forty million innocent unborn human beings since abortion was legalized in 1973. It is hard to imagine a more massive rebellion against God's law than this. The blood of these innocents cries to heaven for justice. What will a mother who has contracted with a doctor to murder her child, or the doctor himself, say on Judgment Day? Will they assert their "rights" to Jesus Christ? Do they think the Fifth Commandment doesn't apply to them?

Now is the time for legal abortion to end, and for all who are guilty of it to repent. Now is the time for all true Catholics to stop voting for politicians who approve of abortion — especially when such politicians call themselves Catholic. Now is the time for us to redouble our fasting and prayer in order to combat this great evil.

Now is also the time for all true Catholics to help those who have killed their unborn children to come back to Christ and be reconciled to the Church. Deep inside, these mothers' consciences are tormented; if not, such women are the most pitiable of individuals. Why is this? Though a feeling of guilt for abortion is terrible, it is justified. I *ought* to feel guilty if I have killed my unborn child. But far worse morally are those who have committed this sin and yet feel no guilt. God will forgive any repented sin, but He will not force us to repentance. Let us, through Project Rachel and other ministries, as well as through personal witness and persuasion, lovingly call our misled sisters and their accomplices to forgiveness, peace, and hope. Surely this is part of our vocation.

We must not forget that abortion is the direct, natural, and unavoidable result of contraception. Nor that some forms of contraception are not contraceptive at all, but abortifacient. That is, they don't prevent conception, they cause abortion. Popes Pius XI and Paul VI were right about the horrible results of the acceptance of contraception. These vicars of Christ foresaw the devaluation of human life, the disintegration of marriage, the rise of divorce and marital infidelity, and other evils that result from contraception. We know more now. We know that contraception has encouraged a massive epidemic of venereal disease among teenagers. We now understand that the promiscuity fostered by contraception has led to millions of divorces. These in turn have led to millions of families headed only by a mother. Such families, sadly, contribute a high percentage of gang members and sociopaths to the underside of our society. In fact, *the whole malaise of family life today, and the problems to which it leads, are caused at least in part by contraception.*

Modern contraception is, of course, a product of technology.

As technology has leapt forward, so has the ability to break the Fifth Commandment. Killing children *in utero* has become easier and less physically traumatic as new machines and drugs have developed. Other forms and goals of killing the innocent have joined abortion. Often enough, this new easy murder is cultivated as something charitable and good. Strangely, the forces of the culture of death in Western society almost always justify their killing of the innocent as a form of "compassion."

What are some specifics of this charge? First, many people urge the use of embryonic stem cells in research for medicines. But we cannot morally resort to this use. Killing unborn human beings so as to harvest medical ingredients from them is gravely wrong, and no true good can come of it. This is true whether the embryos are formed by cloning or by the combination of sperm and ova. Compassion for the sick cannot morally lead to killing the innocent. What's more, as of this writing, *no cure at all for any disease* has been developed from embryonic stem cells. This is true in spite of years of effort. By contrast, *adult* stem cells (such as those found in bone marrow) have produced effective treatments for more than seventy ailments. It would be wrong to destroy the innocent for medical ingredients even if such destruction were the only method; but it is doubly wrong when a morally licit source is so easily available — even in our own bones and noses.

Second, the movement in favor of euthanasia — "nice death" — has grown stronger with the years. But the deliberate killing of old and helpless people, *even with their consent*, is against the law of God. True, we are not obliged to use extraordinary means of treatment to keep people alive. But artificially giving food and water to comatose patients is not extraordinary any more. Some would even say that water and nutrition are not "treatment," since they are not medicine. They address no symptoms except hunger and thirst. Nevertheless, cutting off food and water is now the most frequently used method of killing inconvenient patients — always in the supposed pursuit of compassion. Needless to say, when such a method is used, the patient dies at the hands of the doctor and family, not from any disease. Though such killing often occurs at the hands of misled loved ones, by the law of God it is still murder.

Jesus also teaches through the Church that suicide violates the Fifth Commandment. It is immoral to kill yourself. Since most self-killing, in the Church's current view, is committed by people who are not fully responsible for their actions, suicides can now receive the benefits of a funeral Mass and be buried in sacred ground. Nevertheless, the public approval of suicide is a distressing feature of the culture of death. The euthanasia movement has festered in some countries to the point where many people now arrange for their own self-murder. "Doctor-assisted suicide" is legal even in part of the United States now. This atrocity is also sold as a form of compassion. But its acceptance depends upon the rejection of suffering, rather than acceptance and trust in God. By both His teaching and His self-sacrifice, Jesus teaches that suffering has value when we accept it as God intends. Where are we headed? In our flight from accepting the cross, what depths of sin — despair and pride and mass murder — lie ahead?

To return to the relationship between anger and murder. The Lord taught that all the Ten Commandments are permanently binding. He also deepened them so that they no longer refer only to external actions but to internal states. Accordingly, the Church extends the meaning of the Fifth Commandment beyond deeds to thoughts. Jesus taught that hatred is murder in the heart. Thus He also teaches that the person who *cultivates* anger and hatred is, internally, a murderer — guilty of breaking the Fifth Commandment.

Seen merely as an emotion, anger is blameless. Emotions

are part of our human nature. Fear and anger, sympathy and affection, repulsion and attraction: these movements of the soul occur unbidden. They don't come from our will. Therefore, it is not the origin or beginning of anger that breaks the moral law. It is when we deliberately hold on to anger — and even more, when we harden it into hatred and express it in word and deed — that anger becomes the spiritual equivalent of murder.

On the positive side, the Church teaches that every Catholic has the serious obligation to foster peace. This means, first, that we ask Christ to reign in our hearts and minds — that we pray to God, "Thy Kingdom come" within us. Second, it means that when we can do so, we bring the peace of order, forgiveness, and mutually respectful discussion to strife-filled situations. Thus we become instruments of God's grace. We should always remember the obligations expressed in the "Prayer of St. Francis": "Lord, make me a channel of your peace."

We are to pray for our enemies. We are to conquer evil with good. If we want forgiveness from God, we must forgive people who wrong us. We must banish resentment from our hearts, for resentment is the opposite of forgiveness. When ill will rises again in our minds after we have made an effort to forgive, we must make the effort again. God knows that we are human and that human passions assail us even when we try to rise above them. But with Christ's help we can break the cycle of injury-revenge-injury by meeting injury with forgiveness. Thus we can become the peacemakers who are the true children of God. Thus will we better resemble the Prince of Peace.

Have I kept the Fifth Commandment?

1. Have I entertained murderous thoughts about anyone?
2. Have I deliberately remained angry at someone?
3. Have I refused to forgive anyone who has wronged me?

4. Am I estranged from any member of my own family? Have I tried to end this separation?
5. Have I devalued my own life?
6. Have I had an abortion, or encouraged someone else to have one?
7. Have I been on the pro-life side of today's political debates? Or have I supported abortion, the destruction of human embryos for medical purposes, or the legal encouragement of suicide?
8. Have I killed anyone? Have I taken pleasure from anyone's death?

Commandment 6
You Shall Not Commit Adultery.

Again, the teaching of the Church includes much more than the commandment seems to say. Adultery in the narrow sense is only one of the sexual sins forbidden by the Sixth Commandment. Even from ancient times, before the New Testament was written, this commandment was understood to include a whole array of sins of the flesh. The Church has continued this interpretation. Along with adultery, the Sixth Commandment forbids fornication, masturbation, bestiality, and other sins. It also forbids the popular sin of contraceptive use, and the increasingly stylish sin of sodomy. It not only forbids acts, however, but sexual sins of thought. "Adultery," in the teaching of Christ, includes the sin of lust. The Sixth Commandment is closely related to the Ninth. The Ninth Commandment forbids *desiring* someone else's wife or husband; such a desire is one type of covetousness, which is wholly a sin of *thinking* — wanting something that belongs to another. Both the Sixth Commandment and the Ninth Commandment include this sin.

Adultery and lust. We all know what adultery is. It is sexual activity between a married woman and a man who is not her husband, or between a married man and a woman who is not his wife. This sin was considered so horrid in Old Testament times that the punishment for it was death by stoning. However, when Jesus was confronted with the opportunity to authorize this dire punishment in the person of a woman who had been caught committing adultery, He pointed out that the universality of sin should dissuade people from mob violence. He admonished the crowd — "Let him who is without sin cast the first stone" — and also the woman — "Go and sin no more" (cf. John 8: 3-11). Jesus thus brought mercy to this serious sin of weakness. We may rejoice that He brings the same to us when we repent. Thank God for the mercy He has shown us in Christ. If we didn't have it, we would all be condemned.

Adultery would not require mercy if it were not seriously sinful. But Jesus also teaches that *lust* is a form of adultery. Any man who looks at a woman lustfully, He says, "has already committed adultery with her in his heart" (Matthew 5:28). The teaching of the Lord is clear: such lust, or desire to commit adultery, is the moral equivalent of adultery accomplished.

In framing this principle, Christ elucidates the age-old revealed teaching against divorce. When He is asked if a man may divorce his wife, He responds that a divorced person who marries commits adultery. As far as the Church is concerned, a legal divorce from one's wife or husband does not really dissolve a valid marriage. "What God has joined," the marriage rite says, "man may not divide." The Church has always taught that divorce is objectively impossible (just as she teaches that homosexual "marriage" is impossible.)

Nevertheless, as civil divorce has risen among Catholics

(hand-in-hand with their acceptance of contraception), the Church has honed a procedure for examining individual marriages in their origin to determine if they were valid in the first place. We call this procedure the annulment process. When a marriage is found to have been defective in its origins, it is declared null. It must be emphasized that the purpose of the annulment process is to *preserve* Christ's teaching on matrimony, while allowing civilly divorced Catholics to ascertain whether they are free to marry. In spite of much abuse of the annulment process, it is not, as sometimes charged, the equivalent of "Catholic divorce." An annulment is not a statement of divorce. It is a statement that no real marriage ever existed. And, to repeat, its purpose is to honor and preserve the sacrament of matrimony.

No one should take the idea of annulment lightly. No one should assume that freedom to marry is automatically granted. One must approach the annulment process with humility and acceptance of whatever the tribunal decides.

Anyone who is currently divorced and yet living in a sexual relationship is committing adultery and therefore violating the Sixth Commandment. This is what Scripture and the Church teach. This is true even if the couple have undergone a civil marriage or a marriage in some non-Catholic communion. If you are in such a relationship, you should see a priest or deacon about getting right with the Church. The Church will welcome your inquiry with open arms, just as the father in the Gospel welcomed the prodigal son. It is quite possible that you will be able to have your present marriage validated in the Church. With this blessing, you can again receive the Lord in Holy Communion. You can also set the right example for your children. You can rejoice at your membership in the Body of Christ.

Fornication. Fornication is sexual relations between unmarried people. It overlaps with adultery when a married person has sexual relations with an unmarried one. Fornication is strongly encouraged in sex-education classes in many of our schools. Fornication is almost a way of life at many of our universities, where recreational sex is as common and routine as tooth-brushing — alas, even in some Catholic universities. Only the strongest young Christian can withstand the temptation and peer pressure. What's more, the sexual practices of many very young people — even when they don't involve actual copulation, or "sex" in the traditional sense — are the equivalent of fornication. We are, I believe, at a crisis stage in the miseducation of our youth. Catholic parents should not be so naïve as to think that their children have not heard of these things. In accord with the teaching of Scripture and the Church, they must teach chastity to their children. It is for certain that public schools won't. In fact, some "abstinence" education leaves room for a very active and very sinful sex life.

No matter your age, if you have been guilty of fornication, Jesus calls you back to friendship with Him and His Mother. No matter what you have done, after the sacrament of Penance you will be white as snow. Return to Him with all your heart now.

Pornography. Sadly, the pornography industry has grown into a multibillion-dollar business in the United States, and its corruption is spread around the world. The Anglican writer C.S. Lewis said that when the human appetites fell, sex must have fallen the farthest. He was right. No human need or desire has been so degraded as human sexuality. No human good has been so misused. Satan well knows how to use the inordinate human preoccupation with sex — that is, lust — to his own advantage.

The appeal of pornography is nothing but indulgence of the lust that Jesus condemns. Its essence is fantasized sexual relations, guided by pictures and sound, with people to whom one is not married. In pornography, people — usually women — are degraded to the status of objects. The fact that they participate willingly, for money, does not lessen the sin. In fact, it increases it. Porn "stars" make whole careers of being *non-persons* for the depraved advantage of anonymous masturbators. While the lust for pornography is indulged, it is never appeased. That is why the best customers for "adult" businesses are addicts: they seek ever-new images for sexual excitement. Like other addictions, their habit must be fed regularly. Sadly, pornography addicts burn alluring and degrading images indelibly into their minds, and can scarcely ever remove them.

That is why they need divine help. With the help of frequent confession and regular Mass attendance, a pornography user can help the sewage in his mind fade away. He can break the habit of indulging this addiction. It may be that he will need professional counseling from a solidly Catholic psychologist. He may need to join a twelve-step group. If so, let him seek these gifts from God and receive them gladly. He will be eternally grateful that he did. And while he makes the effort, let him never forget that the Son of God is ready to help and forgive; that the Mother of God will lend the love of her Immaculate Heart to the effort.

But what *is* pornography? Don't forget that, in this sad time of Western cultural decay, much of the entertainment that comes to our houses by way of television is sexually explicit, or sexually suggestive, or based on an immoral worldview. It is pornographic, though almost no one thinks so. *Pornography* has been so narrowly defined that we don't recognize how pornographic the mainstream media have become. Because the legal definition of pornography is limited to the actual depiction of genitals and genital activity, we fail to see the pornography all around us. But in any moral definition, what is really and truly pornographic is now in full view even in grocery stores, and on TV and movie screens.

Many movies made for general consumption can be easily used as pornography. It seems that many movie producers try for an "R" rating in order to lure more viewers. The problem is progressive. Constant dwelling upon violent and oversexed films renders wholesome entertainment too bland. Viewers of all ages become jaded and, like the pornography addict, want stronger and stronger images of depravity. In addition to movies, many of the cable channels are soaked through with immorality; MTV comes to mind. It takes strong resolution, and a truly adult aspiration for self-reform, to stop consuming the sexual immorality found on TV. But Jesus will help anyone who confesses to repent and change his habits of living.

Masturbation. This sin is self-directed, contraceptive sexual activity. It is by definition self-gratification. It violates the constant moral teaching of the Church which restricts sexual activity to self-*giving* in marriage. Furthermore, it often involves the use of pornography, which transforms human beings from persons into mere objects. Persons bear the image of God; mere objects cannot. Also, masturbation almost always involves sinful fantasies even when it doesn't include pornography. The Church has always taught that masturbation is gravely wrong.

Contraception. It is said that nearly all Catholics have accepted the use of contraception into their marriages. Even those who are not married have learned to depend upon contraception as an apparent way of escaping the consequences of their sin. Small wonder that Catholic marriage has become so frail. In modern times, divorce is as common among Catholics as among non-Catholics.

Contraception contributes to this evil in many ways. It makes adultery easy. It also helps young people to think they can fornicate without consequence before marriage. Another toxin comes with this poison practice: When young people come to believe that fornication is okay, they automatically accept the liceity of sex outside marriage. Since this false belief doesn't go away at the altar, they enter marriages more or less ready to commit adultery. An evil conscience is not negated by a vow. That is one reason that "trial marriages" are such a failure. Contraception also reduces men and women from potentially fruitful co-creators in God's Kingdom to temporarily sterile sex objects. Pope Paul VI was right when he wrote in *Humanae Vitae* that the acceptance of contraception leads to all kinds of moral ills, including the destruction of marriage.

On an individual basis, contraception prevents the complete self-giving that is a necessary component of true marriage. It is meaningless to say "I love you" if the "you" has to be altered through chemical or mechanical sterilization. In this case, self-giving is short-circuited because the self is reduced for sexual use. Even worse, wherever contraception has been accepted, legal abortion has followed. It seems that a denial of the goodness of children must include all means of avoiding them.

If births must be spaced — and this should be decided only on the basis of good reasons — the Church teaches that natural family planning is a licit way to space them. NFP is just as effective as any contraception. But it does not involve the rejection of God's good creation. Rather, it represents a cooperation with that creation. Any Catholic couple accustomed to contraception should resolve to take the Church's teaching on this grave matter seriously. Natural family planning offers a practical, morally licit, marriage-enhancing alternative to the gravely sinful practice of contraception.

Finally, contraception has contributed powerfully to the epidemic of venereal disease among teenagers. Current research shows that *eight thousand* teenagers are diagnosed with a sexually transmitted disease in this country *every day*. These are the same young people who have been taught how to get and use contraceptives. This teaching has led them to promiscuity, with disastrous results.

Sodomy. As all the world knows, the chorus of homosexual

activists has become deafening; in many circles, the voices of reason and Scriptural morality are drowned out. Against the nature of mankind and the teaching of Jesus, arrogant governments have assumed the power even to redefine marriage. But "homosexual marriage" will always remain an anti-Christian fantasy. Two men, or two women, can never truly marry.

Yet the Church teaches that all human beings, no matter what their inclinations, are to be treated with respect. All are immortal. All will spend eternity either with God or without Him. So the Church must welcome, minister to, and help all who turn to her.

Those who are inclined to homosexuality should seek out counselors and psychologists who have successfully treated this problem. Many homosexuals have been cured as a result of effort, prayer, and counseling (though the aggressive homosexual lobby denies this fact). There is an excellent organization within the Catholic Church that helps people who are homosexual or confused about their sexuality to live chastely. This organization is called Courage. It is not to be confused with other organizations that deny the moral law and the tradition of the Church; such groups as Dignity reject the Church's teaching and demand that it be changed. They don't understand that the moral teaching of the Church is a reflection of *reality*, not a subjectively derived set of rules that can be changed at will.

God will be merciful to anyone who turns to Him. Confession and penance will help those with homosexual urges to fight those desires, just as God helps heterosexuals who turn to Him for help to fight the lust of the flesh.

Bestiality, polygamy, "polyamory," pedophilia, etc. Sexual deviancy has been defined down so that now, to some people, almost nothing is deviant. Without going into explanations, however, it is easy to see that these practices are at war with the Christian concept of the family — with the teaching of Christ in the Scriptures and the Sacred Tradition of the Church. Any experiment with any of these sexual practices is gravely wrong and should be confessed.

To summarize: The Sixth Commandment forbids all sexual activity, as well as deliberately cultivated sexual desire, except between a man and a woman who are duly married to each other. In a society that is awash in sexual sin, we need God's special help to remain chaste. The sacrament of Penance offers such help.

Have I kept the Sixth Commandment?

1. Have I engaged in sexual activity of any sort with a person to whom I am not married?
2. Have I looked at someone to whom I am not married with lust in my heart?
3. Have I used pornography of any kind? Am I tempted by Internet porn? Do I perceive the pornographic and evil nature of much of the "mainstream" media?
4. Have I engaged in contraceptive sex?
5. Have I masturbated?

COMMANDMENT 7
You shall not steal.

Stealing in its simplest form first comes to mind. If I take something that doesn't belong to me, I violate the Seventh Commandment. But most of the content of the word *stealing* is more complicated. The Church over the years — particularly since the Industrial Revolution — has greatly expanded her reflections on the nature of stealing. All kinds of theft, robbery, and fraud were included in the traditional definition, which is summarily given in the *Catechism of the Council of Trent*. With the later advent of industrialized nations and a new awareness of attendant social problems, the Church paid new attention to poverty, economic fairness, and responsible stewardship. The result has been the growth, since the late nineteenth century, of the "social teaching" of the Church. Most of this teaching falls under the Seventh Commandment. All of it asserts the dignity of the human person against acts and structures that disregard that dignity.

If I take someone else's property without permission or purchase, I violate the Seventh Commandment. If I take money for work that I do not conscientiously perform, I steal my wages. If I am an employer who pays less than the hard work of my employees is worth, I am stealing their labor and committing a serious injustice against my workers and their families. (Although the rate of pay is determined largely by market forces, employers should treat their workers with charity and fairness. In our modern consumer society, those who think they must have all the amenities usually need at least two moderate salaries just to get along. Perhaps we really need less, demand too much, and give too little to the poor.)

In a related matter, several areas of the world are still plagued by the practice of human slavery and related offenses. Those who enslave other human beings are sinning grievously against the Seventh Commandment. A subset of this: those who force young people into prostitution — a practice far too common in much of the world, and supported by evil immoralists from wealthy nations — steal from God's children their virtue, their health, their hope, and their very lives. For such robbers and thieves hell was created.

An example from a more everyday level. If I am given too much change and don't give it back, I steal it. Here is a little tale that was recently circulated. A new priest was sent to a town where he wasn't known. In street clothes, he rode a bus. When he paid the fare, he was given too much change. As he sat in the back of the bus, he considered whether he would return the money. He thought it didn't matter, since the sum was trifling and the sin involved in keeping it would be venial. But finally, he decided to return the change. When he approached the driver and returned the few cents that he owed, the driver said, "Thank you, Father. Yes, I know who you are. You're the new priest at St. Francis de Sales Church. I was testing you."

Since we never know what our influence will be, we should be scrupulously honest. It is rare indeed when we sincerely don't know what belongs to us and what doesn't belong. Whether people are watching us or not, God always is. We should act with this fact in mind.

Do I cheat on my income taxes? If so, I violate the Seventh Commandment (and also the eighth, which forbids lying). Another anecdote: A man got the oil changed in his car, and also asked to have a new air filter installed. When the time came to pay the bill, the air filter wasn't included. He told the clerk about it, and the clerk was surprised; so few people would have been so honest. The customer said, "God knows I got it." And the clerk enjoyed telling that exemplary story for a long time thereafter. One man's responsible honesty thus became a public example.

When the supermarket makes a mistake in my favor, do I say anything, or do I just take the bargain? Have I tried to sell anything while hiding its defects? Have I refused to pay a bill for something that I agreed to buy? Am I looking for someone to sue in order to get money that I haven't earned? In all my dealings with others, do I strive for honesty?

These are everyday moral situations in which the Seventh Commandment is most frequently broken. The larger situations — the unjust social and governmental structures about which the Church frequently talks — are in general beyond the individual's power to change. Nevertheless, we can speak up when we see injustice. And we can engage in private charitable giving, such as that encouraged by the Church. In fact, we must do so. The tsunami of 2004 in the Indian Ocean comes to mind. No amount of government money could have made up for the help rendered by private charities, including the Church.

The Church firmly upholds the right of private property as a precondition to true stewardship. How is it possible to be fully responsible for something one doesn't own? And yet the Church also teaches that the universal end of created goods is the human family at large, and not merely the rich segments of that family. God truly owns everything we have. All is lent to us so that we can use it in His service.

The Church upholds the capitalist principle — that people are entitled to own property, make money, and use their possessions as they choose. Because money itself is productive and not merely a symbolic medium of exchange, charging moderate interest is not immoral. But the Church is also aware that people in many parts of the world need help to realize their human potential. Such measures as will aid them to become productive, to join in the cycle of production and trade, and to move toward a better standard of living should be a goal of our foreign policy. At the same time, when natural disaster or hopeless poverty devastates a people or nation, we should realize that we are obligated to render such aid as we can through charitable organizations or the Church. In fact, *almsgiving has always been recognized as a positive obligation* under the Seventh Commandment. The Scriptures make it quite clear that no one who callously sits on possessions while other people suffer from want will enter the Kingdom of Heaven. Remember Christ's parable of the rich man and the beggar (Luke 16:19-31).

Caution is necessary, however. We should use discretion in giving alms. The Church urges us to plan our giving — to purpose in our hearts and put aside generous gifts to the Church and to the poor. Jesus teaches that the pursuit of perfection involves giving all we have to the poor (cf. Matthew 19:21). But not every generous act has good results. We are assailed on all sides these days by able-bodied people who claim to be sick, to be veterans, to be looking for work. It is a fact that many of these beggars are addicted to drugs, including alcohol, and that a gift of money would not be a real help. It would, instead, prolong their real troubles.

It is not a sin to withhold money from people who will poison themselves with it. In fact, giving an addict money enables him to destroy himself. For this reason, most of our giving should probably be through the Church and through other private charities that we know will not misuse our contributions. Not to give at all, however, is gravely sinful. So if we err, we should err on the side of generosity. We must always remember that when we give real help to the needy, we give it to Jesus Himself.

The Seventh Commandment has a further moral requirement. Sacred Tradition requires restitution of stolen property. In the Old Testament, the psalmist asks, "Must I restore what I did not steal?" (Psalm 69:5, New American Bible). The answer is No. But that answer clearly implies an answer of Yes to the alternate question, "Must I restore what I stole?" When possible, we must pay back what we have taken. When this is not possible, we must make *some* kind of reparation. If those whom we have treated unjustly are out of reach before we repent — if they are dead, or if we don't know where they live — we should pray for them and give alms, asking the Lord to accept our offering as reparation for our sin.

Sometimes direct reparation will do more harm than good. The AA code of making "amends" except when they will be harmful is a good guide here. Obviously, if making amends is going to cause further harm, it shouldn't be done. Nevertheless, reparation must be made. In a very real sense, we can spend our lives in the service of God and offer ourselves to the Father in the name of Jesus, all as an offering in sorrow for our sins. Our debt will never be paid. But it is still a good idea to make specific offerings for specific remembered sins.

Have I kept the Seventh Commandment?

1. Have I taken something that doesn't belong to me? If so, I must not only confess the sin, but must do my best to restore that which I stole. I will follow my priest-confessor's advice about restitution.
2. Have I been stingy and unfair toward employees? Have I stolen their labor? Have I respected them as persons created in God's image?
3. Have I defrauded anyone through an unjust lawsuit or through other means? Have I borrowed money and not paid it back, or made debts that I didn't repay?
4. Have I been honest in my tax returns?
5. Do I give generously to the poor and to the Church? Do I give enough? Is my giving only from my excess, or does it necessitate self-denial? I should remember the poor widow in the New Testament, who gave generously in her poverty and was praised by Jesus (Mark 12:41-44).
6. Have I, through prayer and almsgiving, tried to help the world's underprivileged people?
7. Is my faith in my mind only, or does it translate itself into charity toward others — such charity as God has shown me?

Commandment 8
You shall not bear false witness against your neighbor.

Why is *lying* gravely sinful, even a mortal sin? Because God is Truth. When we lie, we make ourselves foreign to God. When we lie, we associate ourselves with Satan, who is "a liar and the father of lies."

The Eighth Commandment prohibits all kinds of speech designed to deceive others. This is its negative aspect. It also has positive aspects, however — the obligation to tell the truth, and the obligation to make reparation for the harm caused by one's lies.

The first kind of speech prohibited by this commandment is literal false witness, whether in a court of law or outside of one. If I accuse someone falsely of a crime, or if I fail to defend someone whom I know to be innocent, I sin against the Eighth Commandment. Probably most instances of false witness in our society occur in civil cases. Of all societies that have ever existed, ours is the most devoted to lawsuits. Many of these suits are without merit, based solely on the fact that trial lawyers want to make a lot of money while pretending to stand up for plaintiff's "rights." Many more occur because some people are always looking for someone to sue, in order to get money that they haven't earned. The contemptible combination of ambulance-chasing lawyers advertising on television with viewers who are looking for easy money is all too familiar.

Though some plaintiffs have indeed suffered needlessly and greatly, and are therefore entitled to remuneration, many are lured into litigation by lawyers. Even those who have been seriously injured are not entitled to be made rich at society's expense. For someone who hasn't been genuinely and unfairly injured to allege injury so as to get money is surely a grievous offense against the Eighth Commandment. Unfortunately, this happens all the time. In the aftermath of discoveries about asbestos, for instance, many people *suffering from no injury at all* have received money from unjustified lawsuits. Meanwhile, the suits have driven many companies out of business, thus causing the loss of thousands of jobs and harm to thousands of families.

Another serious breach of the Eighth Commandment is known as *detraction*. This sin does not involve lying. Rather it occurs when we tell bad *truths* about people that are not necessary to tell. Note that in this case even truth-telling is forbidden by the Eighth Commandment. Remember that if it is not necessary to say something bad about someone, it *is* necessary *not* to say it. The related sin of *slander* occurs when we say *false* bad things about others. The harm here is obvious. But whether the charges are true or false, the point is that you and I don't need to go around saying what's wrong with other people. If someone has a fault, you don't need to point it out. We need to focus especially on our own faults.

Both slander and detraction are the subject matter of *gossip*. The temptation to talk about other people — to "take their inventory," as the jargon of Alcoholics Anonymous puts it — is very strong and very evil. "A whisperer defiles his own soul and is hated in his neighborhood," the book of Sirach teaches. The psalmist records his effort to "bridle [his] mouth" (Psalm 39:1) — an effort that we should all make. No one who doesn't really need to know should be told how bad your mother-in-law or your pastor or your neighbor is. And no one should ever be lied about.

Many Catholics today — people who, at any rate, call themselves Catholics — think it is their duty to criticize the Church. In particular, those who think the Church is backward in matters of sexual morality, marriage, divorce, clerical celibacy,

Examination of Conscience in Light of the Ten Commandments

Confession, contraception, and a host of popular sins, demand that the Church change. Slander against the Church is prominent in our entertainment culture. Just a few short decades ago, the Catholic Church was generally treated with respect in popular entertainment such as movies. One need think only of *The Bells of St. Mary's* and other such Hollywood products, which exhibited genuine piety. I myself was deeply attracted to the Church when, as a child, I saw the reverence extended to the altar by characters in movies — such a reverence as would have been nonsense in my own altarless church. Though I didn't come to the Church until decades later, I sensed the holiness of the tabernacle where Jesus stayed. Now, however, the majority of cinematic references to the Church are attacks on Catholic faith and practice. Now, we see priests derided as sodomites, pedophiles, and fools, as worldly exploiters of others, as hypocrites who don't even believe what the Church teaches. Meanwhile, faithful Catholics are ridiculed. The Hollywood Church of the present is usually evil and inhumane, and the Hollywood history of the Church is twisted into falsehood.

Books are similar in their false representation. There are endless examples of lying fiction and falsified history that slander the Church. Bizarre falsehoods about Jesus and Mary Magdalene, slanders against Pope Pius XII, perversely distorted accounts of Church history — the list goes on.

But these are celebrity products. What can we do about them? Where do we, the little people, stand with relation to our culture? Most of the time we are unable to change the big cultural trends of our society. Decadence continues. Nevertheless, we should refute lies against the Church when we can. We should also be careful not to contribute financially to the propagation of falsehood about the Church: *don't buy these books or see these movies*. Give the money to the poor. Above all, we should keep our spiritual lives in order. Our reverent attendance at Mass, the moral probity of our lives, and our constancy in prayer and service to others will bear fruit for Christ. Thus will we counteract the popular slanders against Christ's Church.

Detraction has a companion: lies told to ingratiate oneself with others. As the catechisms of the Church make clear, such *affirmative* speech can also be false witness. Flattery, for instance. To praise a vain boss in order to get a promotion is to lie. The office "brown-noser" is as much a liar as the office gossip. The lickspittle who fawns on his college professor in order to make a good grade is as much a liar as someone who spreads false rumors about his professor. It seems there are many ways to bear false witness, and all of them are infractions against the Eighth Commandment.

Finally, however, we should note that we are not always obliged to tell all the truth. We often need to hold our tongues. If your mother on her deathbed says, "My hair is a mess," and you say "Mother, you look great," you have done the right thing. Sometimes the whole truth can cause unbearable pain or disaster. On such occasions, one is not obliged to tell all. In a classic example, the great Dr. Johnson of English literary fame clearly implies that one need not tell the truth when a murderer asks "which way the man went." Often our only guide is charity, which comes from God.

Reparation for breaking the Eighth Commandment is required. It may range from an apology to financial restitution, depending upon the harm done by one's speech. It's hard to imagine a proper restitution for a lie that sent someone to jail for years — such might be the result of false witness — but the effort would have to be made. Whatever you have done, listen to your priest-confessor's recommendations about restitution.

Examination of Conscience in Light of the Ten Commandments

Have I kept the Eighth Commandment?

1. Have I lied about someone else?
2. Have I betrayed a confidence?
3. Have I committed the sin of detraction by pointing out someone's faults when I didn't have to?
4. Have I broken a promise?
5. Have I taken part in an unjustified lawsuit?
6. Do I wholeheartedly accept the teaching authority of the Church and treat her with respect, or do I call myself Catholic while demanding that the Church change her teachings?
7. Have I tried to make amends for the lies I have told?

COMMANDMENT 9
You shall not covet your neighbor's wife.

The Ninth and Tenth Commandments are especially important because they forbid sins of *thought*. In doing so, they clearly foreshadow the teaching of Jesus. The thought involved in both is called "concupiscence." This word denotes an immoral desire. In terms of these two commandments, concupiscence is a desire to possess something belonging to someone else. Hence in the Catholic tradition the Ninth Commandment forbids the desire for your neighbor's wife or husband; and the Tenth forbids the desire for your neighbor's property.

Like the Sixth Commandment, the Ninth pertains to the sin of adultery. But whereas the Sixth is mainly about the sinful *acts* that fall under the heading of adultery, the Ninth is about the *thought* of adultery. The Ninth is more about lust, a mental act. The Lord Jesus included the prohibitions of both commandments when He stated that merely looking upon a woman to lust after her is equivalent to the act of adultery. For Him adultery and *consent* to adultery are not morally distinct.

We should be aware that any intentional desire to commit a sinful act is itself sinful. This doesn't mean that we sin when the possibility of sinning flits across our minds. It is when we turn a mere possibility into a concupiscent desire by holding on to it that our thoughts become sinful. To know that sexual sin exists, and to know what it looks like, do not constitute sin. But to *wish* that one could commit some of the sexual sins forbidden by the Sixth Commandment is in itself immoral. Also, to look back with longing on a missed opportunity to sin is itself sinful. That money that could have been easily stolen; that person with whom fornication would have been easy: such memories become sinful when they become objects of desire; when missed sin comes to look like lost opportunity. We must ask God to help us eject such thoughts permanently from our minds. To wish to sin is sinful.

Thus the last two commandments point forward to the teaching of the Messiah. They reflect the internal conflict that was started with the first sin, and they are echoed in the Savior's thoughts. When Jesus preaches that the "pure of heart… shall see God" (Matthew 5:8), He is noting the reward that accompanies victory over our lower urges. Such a victory, as the *Catechism* teaches, is not possible without the Holy Spirit's help. So the pure of heart are already in the sanctifying care of God, and they live lives that already partake of heaven.

It is striking that Jesus' contemporaries — the ones who rejected Him and ultimately had Him crucified — seem to have missed the significance of these last two commandments. They seem not to have known about sins of thought. All of their religion was external and legalistic. Their virtues were open acts done so that others could admire them. The only sins they seem to have recognized were sins of external omission or commission

— obligatory acts such as tithing that they failed to accomplish, or sinful acts such as theft or blasphemy that they did commit. But Jesus, who created the human mind and will, knows the depths from which sin springs. He knows that the guilt of sin attaches to intentions deep within the heart, not merely to acts visibly done or undone. Furthermore, He extended our moral responsibility to encompass our relations with all mankind. Such was His definition of "neighbor."

The conflict between what we know to be right and the lower urges of our human hearts came into being at the Fall. Before the time when Adam and Eve sinned against God, the human heart was in perfect accord with His will; the battle between what one knows to be right and what one desires to do had not begun. When sin came in, the condition of "original innocence" was replaced by original guilt and shame, as Pope John Paul II taught in *The Theology of the Body*. The resulting conflict — the struggle in the mind between knowledge of what is right and desire for what is wrong — is powerfully described by St. Paul (in Romans 7). It is a constant feature of our fallen human nature.

They are blessed who perceive this conflict in themselves. Those who don't perceive it often have scarred and useless consciences — mere permission machines that approve of all they want to do. Such people are to be pitied and prayed for, for their spiritual peril is great. Not only do they sin (like everyone), but they do so without any worry.

The psalmist David, in his great hymn of penitence (Psalm 51), begs: "Create a clean heart in me, O God." The author of Psalm 24 asks, "Who can ascend the mountain of the Lord, or who may stand in his holy place?" And then he answers his own question: "He whose hands are sinless, whose heart is clean." Jesus Christ teaches that the "pure of heart... will see God." It seems that all through salvation history, writers inspired by the

Holy Spirit have seen that both the deeds of the hand and the thoughts of the heart must be given to God to be purified. We cannot work this purification ourselves, for it is from our own fallen wills that evil desires come. Only God can help us here. But He has promised that He will do so. As Jesus was transfigured on the mountain, He will transform us and restore in us the divine image that we, through our weakness and willful disobedience, have obscured.

Have I kept the Ninth Commandment?

1. Have I looked with lust at someone to whom I am not married? Do I relish looking at others in a sexually charged way? Do I wish I had my neighbor's wife?
2. Has lust determined my choice of entertainment — in movies, magazines, reading; or in the company I keep?
3. Do I indulge myself in what I consider minor sexual sin? Do I deliberately toy around with ideas of sexual pleasure with someone to whom I am not married?

COMMANDMENT 10
You shall not covet anything that is your neighbor's.

The Tenth Commandment, like the Ninth, forbids a sin of thought. It extends the prohibition of concupiscence, or wrongly ordered desire, to all that belongs to others. We would say that the subject is inanimate things, except for the fact that the command forbids desiring servants or even animals that belong to one's neighbor.

The Church treats a desire for someone else's property under the heading of "lust of the eye," parallel to the "lust of the flesh" prohibited by the Sixth and Ninth Commandments. St. John speaks of the threefold lust — the "lust of the flesh, the lust of the eyes, and the pride of life" (1 John 2:16) — and Pope John Paul II discusses these various forms of concupiscence in *The Theology of the Body*.

Avarice and envy are particular sins of thought that fall under the Tenth Commandment. Avarice is the desire for wealth and its trappings for their own sake. Merely wanting to make money is innocent, as long as one remembers what money is for. If we hoard it, or seek to make more of it just to aggrandize ourselves, we are clearly "laying up treasure for ourselves on earth," not in heaven. Jesus is very clear in His teaching about this. "Where your treasure is, there will your heart be also," He declares (Luke 12:34). An inordinate love of money and worldly "success" automatically involves a violation both of the first of the Ten Commandments and of the First Great Commandment in the teaching of Christ — that commandment to "love the Lord your God with all your heart" (Matthew 22:37).

Unless we use our money for the common good — for the charities of the Church or other almsgiving, for the rightful care and education of our own families, for projects that will benefit someone besides ourselves — we are misusing it. How many times do we see, in this wealthy country, people building huge houses for themselves and living in them with only a wife or husband, a dog, and maybe one child? Do we not realize that such expenditure of wealth on ourselves, when people are starving and living in squalor, reflects a disordered desire for worldly riches and display?

And — coming to *envy* — how many times do we see our friends and fellow citizens living richly and wish that we had such possessions? Sometimes it seems, in the richest era of the richest country in history, that all of one's friends are rich. They live in huge houses, drive huge cars, and seem able to buy whatever they want. It is hard at times not to let such deceptive realities turn into temptations: *They* have a house where people love to attend large parties, *they* have a swimming pool, *their* only child has his own fully stocked rec room. So, we think, we'll have to get these things. But such thoughts are wrong.

First, note the deceptions of appearance. The chances are good that underneath the surface — concealed within the family's secret knowledge — all these amenities are bought with considerable struggle. Though signs of a life of ease, they may not have been so easily attained. So many people are in such deep debt for the stuff they have. Like the rich fool of the parable, such apparently rich friends may be on the edge of final disaster. And their property has turned into an idol.

Second, we should never let other people's possessions determine what we will buy. "Keeping up with the Joneses" reflects a desire to impress people with *our* possessions, just as the Pharisees of Christ's time wanted to impress people with their public acts of piety. When we are successful at achieving a reputation that we crave, Jesus says, we already have our reward. And it is not in heaven.

Third — again — when we spend extravagantly in order to satisfy an envious desire to keep up with other people, we deprive genuinely poor people of the alms we should give. C.S. Lewis was right when he said that our giving should hurt a bit. If we are perfectly comfortable with what we keep and use, if there is no real sacrifice in our almsgiving, we probably aren't giving enough. The terrible plight of people in such places as Haiti, the poorest country in the Western Hemisphere, should concern us much more than what our neighbors drive or wear.

Classical moralists describe envy as a type of "sadness" — that is, bad feelings because someone else has something that we don't have, or because someone gets something that we don't

Examination of Conscience in Light of the Ten Commandments

get. We are *saddened* because So-and-So drives a Hummer, or because Mr. X was chosen Most Valuable Employee. But such envy is unbecoming to a Christian.

We should sincerely strive to see all that we do in the light of eternity. Such a perspective will help us to know what is truly important and to act accordingly. We will then be able to follow the Christian principle that says we should rejoice in others' successes and share their sorrows with them. Such deference to others requires effort. But more than our own exertion, it requires letting Jesus transform us into His image. For Jesus of Nazareth gave everything and envied no one.

Have I kept the Tenth Commandment?

1. Have I allowed myself to want something that belongs to someone else?
2. Have I let envy determine my desires?
3. Have I let avarice — the desire for wealth in itself — motivate me?
4. Have I skipped Mass unnecessarily in order to pursue business deals (thus breaking the First, the Third, and the Tenth Commandments)?
5. Have I become more of a getter and keeper than a giver to the poor?

A Blessing

It is my sincere prayer that through this book
many will come to know the Lord better. In so doing,
may they become more devoted to the Blessed Virgin, whom
He obeyed on earth and still honors in heaven.
Through their prayers and good works, may they
make reparation to her Immaculate Heart,
which has been so injured by sin and ingratitude.

As the least of deacons, I call upon the greatest of deacons
— St. Stephen, St. Philip, St. Vincent, St. Lawrence,
St. Ephrem, St. Francis, and all in heaven — to join their
prayers to mine. Through their prayers,
and by the grace of Jesus Christ,
may the readers of this book find help in it
to attain their deepest hearts' desire:
eternal life in the presence of the Lord. Amen.